TOXIC
CRITICISM

TOXIC
CRITICISM

BREAK THE CYCLE WITH FRIENDS, FAMILY, COWORKERS, AND YOURSELF

ERIC MAISEL, Ph.D.

New York Chicago San Francisco Lisbon London Madrid Mexico City
Milan New Delhi San Juan Seoul Singapore Sydney Toronto

Library of Congress Cataloging-in-Publication Data

Maisel, Eric, 1947–.
    Toxic criticism : break the cycle with friends, family, coworkers, and yourself /
by Eric Maisel.
        p.   cm.
    Includes bibliographical references and index.
    ISBN 0-07-146555-3
    1. Criticism, Personal.   I. Title.

BF637.C74 M35   2007
158.2—dc22   2006022556

1 2 3 4 5 6 7 8 9 10 11 12 13 14 15 16 17 18 19   FGR/FGR   0 9 8 7 6

ISBN-13: 978-0-07-146555-7
ISBN-10:   0-07-146555-3

McGraw-Hill books are available at special quantity discounts to use as premiums and
sales promotions, or for use in corporate training programs. For more information, please
write to the Director of Special Sales, Professional Publishing, McGraw-Hill, Two Penn
Plaza, New York, NY 10121-2298. Or contact your local bookstore.

This book is printed on acid-free paper.

For Ann

Contents

Acknowledgments

I would like to begin by acknowledging my wife, Ann Mathesius Maisel, to whom all of my books are dedicated, for thirty good years (out of thirty). Then, my thanks to Janet Rosen, my agent, for her support, guidance, wit, and humor, not to mention her sales. Next, my thanks to Natasha Graf, my editor at McGraw-Hill, for wanting this book, championing it, and working to make it better. And to all the folks at the Sheree Bykovsky Agency and at McGraw-Hill who have helped *Toxic Criticism* get a good start out of the gate, a round of applause.

I would also like to thank the many people who joined me in cyberspace as participants in my toxic criticism research group, who responded at length to my questions, provided anecdotes and insights, and shared their "Dear critic" letters. Your contributions have greatly enriched this book and grounded it in human reality. I hope that you benefited from our work together and that you enjoy this book, which in no small measure represents the fruits of your labors.

To my creativity coaching clients in the arts, who know toxic criticism firsthand, I offer heartfelt thanks for the opportunity to work with you over the past twenty years at home and abroad, in workshops, classes, groups, and individually. These have been among my favorite times, and I only hope that the opportunity to work with you and with clients like you continues for many years to come.

Last, I would like to acknowledge my mother, who turned ninety-seven in 2006 and who will complain that the print in this book is too small, no matter what its size. Mom, I know better than to take that criticism personally! I hope that you are still around to pore over this text with your magnifying glass.

Introduction

Examining the Territory of Toxic Criticism

Criticism is a real crippler. I'm sure that you know that—I bet that's why you picked up this book. But you may not be aware just how powerful a negative force criticism can be, how much damage it can do to your self-confidence, or how seriously it can deflect you from your path. Almost nothing does more psychological damage than criticism.

Criticism comes at us from the past, as bad memories and as our own introjected "inner critic." It comes at us every day, at work and at home. It even colors our sense of the future. Some of it is minor and ruffles our feathers only a little bit. But a surprising amount of it is *toxic*, as bad for our system as any poison. *Toxic criticism*, that criticism that gets under our skin and lodges in our mind, can fester like an open wound. It is so devastating a problem that millions of people alter their life plans because of the criticism they suffered as a child, adolescent, or adult. If you want to understand what it takes to regain fortitude in life, you must pay attention to toxic criticism and its profound negative effects.

Every day, as a creativity coach who works with creative and performing artists, I see how toxic criticism affects real people. A writer presents her new idea for a novel to her critique group, the idea is panned, and the writer goes into a monthlong funk. A singer is praised for her performance but receives one offhanded criticism, from her father—and can't schedule new gigs. A painter would love to approach gallery owners with his current paintings but finds it impossible to proceed—he just knows that he's going to get criticized for changing his subject matter. An actor stops auditioning because her "inner critic" has gotten so loud that she doubts her abilities, her chances, her look —everything.

This book is about the terrible toll that criticism takes and what you can do to reduce the effects of it in your life. I will show you what I've learned from working with people who spend their lives on the front lines of criticism—creative and performing artists—and present you with useful ways to deal with it. We'll look at attitude change, cognitive strategies, personality management, existential approaches, and other tactics for handling criticism. Before I present these healing strategies, however, let's get a little more grounded in our subject.

Actual, Anticipated, and Self-Criticism

Criticism falls into three broad categories: *actual criticism, anticipated criticism*, and *self-criticism*. Examples of *actual criticism* are getting a poor job performance review, having your painting attacked in painting class, being held up to ridicule by a sibling, and hearing from a friend that your latest dinner party was your least successful so far. Examples of *anticipated criticism* are worrying what people will say should you present your ideas at work, fearing an attack by critics if your novel gets published, and imagining the critical things your parents will say if you tell them you're thinking of switching careers. Examples of *self-criticism* are demeaning your efforts, calling yourself names, and presuming that you'll never reach your goals.

All three kinds of criticism can have devastating effects. A particular piece of actual criticism can cause you to stop a creative career or decide you aren't good enough to rise to the top of your profession. Your fear of future criticism can cause you to let go of your dreams or not go public with the efforts you make. Your experience of self-criticism can color your days in a negative way, causing you to be more pessimistic and depressed than you otherwise might be—and also more critical. These are three equally toxic poisons, and to eliminate only one from your system isn't enough. You need to break free of all three.

Fair Versus Unfair Criticism

These three brands of criticism come in two flavors: *fair* and *unfair*. It is very important to understand that both "fair criticism" and "unfair criticism" produce toxic effects. If you give a presentation at work for which you didn't prepare and that you deliver poorly, a fair criticism is that your presentation wasn't up to snuff. On the other hand, if you do an excellent job and your boss admonishes you for not starting with a joke, that's unfair criticism. It turns out that *either* criticism can prove toxic—and for *different* reasons.

Fair criticism can prove toxic because it possesses real power to make us angry with ourselves and disappointed in ourselves. We hoped to perform well—and we didn't. We wanted to prove to be excellent leaders—and we didn't. We dreamed that our children would excel—and they didn't. The sting of fair criticism also causes us to fear criticism in the future. Why try again if we're likely to fail and receive more criticism? When fair criticism grows to toxic proportions, it has the cognitive effect of amplifying a truth—that something we did went poorly—

and transforms it into a falsehood, that we are doomed and failures.

Unfair criticism can prove toxic because it makes us angry with other people and with the world. We start to harbor powerful resentments, we begin to doubt the basic integrity and fairness of our fellow human beings, and we entertain the painful possibility that no matter how well we perform "they" will still criticize us. This everyday paranoia causes us to retreat, to lose interest in the things we love, and to sink into a semipermanent depression. We acquire an attitude of "learned pessimism" as a result of being treated unfairly and of "learned helplessness" as a result of having no satisfactory ways to redress the injustice.

Fair criticism can become one sort of toxin and unfair criticism another. What if we get criticized and can't tell in our own mind whether it was fair or unfair? That's the worst! Then we both demean ourselves and rage at others. On top of that, we get to call ourselves additional bad names for not being able to tell whether the criticism was appropriate. The chaos and confusion that result from not being able to determine in our own mind whether a given criticism was fair or unfair weakens us and adds to our sense that we aren't equal to life's demands. Better that the criticism we receive be clearly fair or clearly unfair!

When we fear anticipated criticism, we fear both the fair and the unfair kind. Fair criticism will mean we've made mistakes and messes, and unfair will mean we've been treated unjustly again. Neither is pretty to contemplate. It is not encouraging to picture ourselves failing or attacked for no good reason. The identical situation arises with respect to our "inner critic": some of the criticism we level at ourselves will hurt because it is apt, and some of it will be unfair and will hurt because we sense how unfairly we're treating ourselves.

These are a few of the wrinkles we'll address as we get a handle on the effects of criticism on our system, but let me end this introduction with a story. A client, a world-famous musician, came to me in my capacity as creativity coach. He wanted to take his music in a new direction but didn't feel equal to dealing with the criticism he knew he would receive—from the people around him, from his audience, and from media critics—if he moved his music in this new direction. He'd already grown tremendously in our work together, so much so that he dared contemplate this break with his popular music. But this was a new—and terrifying—precipice for him.

We agreed that he really had no choice in the matter. To grow musically, he had to face his fear of criticism, and he needed to develop new tools to deal with the criticism he was smart enough to know would be coming his way. He couldn't just dash off a "Dear critic" letter (see Chapter 2) to an imaginary critic or add an affirmation to his self-talk vocabulary to prepare himself for this new adventure. He understood that he would have to transform himself into someone who stood in new relationship to the idea of criticism: someone braver, more detached, and all-around savvier.

He did the work outlined in this book. About a month later we chatted on the phone. He explained that he was ready to unveil his new musical ideas to his business manager and to some of his other closest confidants. I asked him if he could explain to me how he'd changed. He replied instantly, "My new mantra is 'I invite criticism.' And I mean it. I've come full circle from fearing it like the devil to opening the door wide. If I don't take risks, I'll die. If I do take risks, people are bound to have plenty of negative things to say. I've nailed that equation in my head." You could hear the new strength in his voice and the new wisdom in his words.

As we proceed, we'll look closely at how criticism transforms itself into negative self-talk, fear of the future, and the emergence of our inner critic. I'll teach you how to handle objectively fair and unfair criticism as well as the kind that falls in between. In reading this book, it is my hope that you'll arrive at a point where most of the criticism directed your way will lose its power to affect you toxically.

To consider

- How do you currently handle criticism?
- How would you like to change your attitude so you are better prepared to handle toxic criticism?
- Based on this initial discussion, which new method(s) would you like to try?

To do

- Please recall an incident of toxic criticism in your life and try to gain clarity about its short-term and long-term effects. If you feel like it, do this exercise in writing.
- As practice, take some risk (like asking for a raise or sending out your latest short story) that invites criticism.

TOXIC
CRITICISM

Part 1

Putting Toxic Criticism in Its Place

1

Understanding the Six Keys

A critical comment can sting only a little, or it can do real harm. The power of criticism to hurt isn't an objective matter. It's not about who delivers it, how nasty it is, or in what circumstances we find ourselves. It's about how we take it in, what it means to us, how it gets a grip on our mind, and the way it eats away at our being. Toxic criticism is the criticism that affects us powerfully, whether or not it was objectively biting, whether or not it was meant to hurt, and whether or not it was even meant as criticism. If it gets inside and does damage, it is toxic.

How We Handle Criticism Ineffectively

Before I identify the six keys for reducing the toxic effects of criticism, I want to look at how people typically—that is, ineffectively—handle the criticism they receive. Our first line of psychological defense with respect to criticism is to try not to hear it—to ignore it somehow. We try our best to not hear caustic comments, notice a snicker or a roll of the eyes, or take in the negative comments penned at the end of our essay. Defending ourselves this way has its pluses—especially if the criticism is unfair—but by resorting to "blindness" we lose out on vital information and put ourselves in danger of repeating our mistakes. We also make ourselves tense and miserable as we try not to hear what people are saying to us. Worse yet, when some piece

3

of criticism manages to get through our defenses, it cuts much more deeply and *really* takes hold.

A second line of defense is to notice the criticism and then get angry with the critic. This method of dealing with criticism strains relationships, makes enemies out of friends and loved ones, and eats away at our insides. We start to live at a simmer or even in a perpetual rage. Millions of seemingly meek people are secretly avenging themselves on their critics, boiling them in oil and tearing them limb from limb. Anger is our most common response to criticism, and because we don't dare vent that anger—it would harm us and others if we turned violent—we live with that anger roiling inside of us, searing our stomach lining.

Internalizing Criticism—Treading a Dangerous Path

Another way we operate is to try to "stuff" the criticism, to take it inside and hide it away as if it were dirty laundry shoved out of sight in a closet. It isn't really out of sight, though—it's as if the closet had no door and a searchlight were permanently trained on the dirty laundry. We obsess about the criticism, prepare responses that we don't deliver, and get caught up in "dealing" with the criticism by never letting it out of our sight. Just as a person with a toothache can't think of anything else, a criticized person trapped in his own mind can think about nothing but the criticism received. This inner pollution feels terrible and is bound to make us sick from one stress-related illness or another.

Another characteristic response to criticism is to take it to heart, feel wounded and diminished, and stop acting in that arena so as not to get criticized again. If the criticism occurred in painting class, we stop painting. If we got criticized about our weight, we stop dating and even stop going out. If our intelligence was attacked, we lower our sights academically. Not only do we not exorcise the criticism, but we let it dictate how we'll live our lives and what we'll consider available to us as options and dreams. The criticism wins—and depression sets in.

Becoming Our Own Critic

Another disturbing way we deal with critical comments is by becoming our own worst critic. No longer is it John in painting class or Mary at work who is passing judgment. We shake our head at our own efforts, declare ourselves unequal to our dreams, and move halfheartedly through life. At this point we've acquired a self-critical style and a way of looking at the world rooted in pessimism, anger, and despair. It is easy to see how criticism that becomes toxic not only affects us moment in and moment out but also ruins our future and transforms the very way we think about ourselves. (I discuss this more in Chapter 4.)

Doubting that the future will be any different from the present, we make a secret pact with ourselves to at least avoid further criticism. We don't date, even though we want love and affection. We don't voice our beliefs or act on our beliefs, even though we have beliefs. We don't stand up for ourselves, even though we know that self-advocacy is the path to success. Even if we understand that we're hiding, we feel powerless to try, since our paramount concern is to avoid getting criticized again. At this point toxic criticism has turned from wound to scar: our future is scarred.

Giving In to Self-Sabotage

Another way we deal with the possibility of future criticism is by sabotaging our efforts. We bravely accept a new position at work, one with more responsibility and more possibility of criticism, and instantly have a car accident. At first glance there might seem to be no connection between the two events. At an unconscious level, however, we may have been looking for a way to avoid the criticism that we know will come with the new job. Panic and a secret wish to undo the decision to move up make us just impulsive enough to try a driving maneuver that we would otherwise never attempt. Did we actually want the accident? No! But maybe. When we fear future criticism, see it looming on the horizon, and don't know how to avoid it, one of the tricks our mind plays is to precipitate an event-ending crisis.

We can also make ourselves sick with worry. If we have a presentation at work that we must give and if we really don't want to sabotage ourselves, we may spend the two weeks before the presentation sick to our stomach, trying to "get it together" but fearing and visualizing the worst. We worry about everything from what we're going to wear to whether the equipment will work on the day of the presentation. Because we are so concerned about the potential for criticism in the situation and because we feel such dread of that criticism, we spend those two weeks in agony.

Sometimes we sabotage ourselves by choosing a path where so little is at stake that no one bothers to pay attention to us. We hide out in a routine civil service job, an uneventful corner of an academic field, or a low-level job devoid of responsibility and scrutiny. Or we become the building inspector who gets to criticize rather than the contractor who must deal with the criticism, the professional critic rather than the artist, or the hypercritical teacher. It may seem odd that a person would pick a profession simply to avoid criticism or to dole it out, but people often select their profession for just such reasons.

Becoming Confrontational

Last but not least, people regularly deal with the specter of future criticism by "acting out" and "getting in the first blow." They become oppositional, let their anger drive their actions, and grow a thick skin to deal with the negative reactions that their acting out provokes. They dress in jeans when they should appear in a suit, stride in with a dirty look, and dare anyone to criticize them for their inappropriate dress. They fail to prepare and then act as if their performance deserves a standing ovation. They become the "difficult" person everyone knows to avoid and not to trust. They inoculate themselves against criticism through narcissistic grandiosity that masks their fear and pain.

None of these methods serves you. As you were never schooled in effectively handling criticism, it's no wonder that you may have little clue about how to deal with it effectively. The following chapters outline a complete, in-depth program for dealing with criticism in healthy ways. By the end of the book you will know exactly what to do to handle unfair and fair criticism, criticism from strangers and from intimates, and direct and indirect criticism—in short, how to handle all the criticism in your life effectively. Let's take our first look at how criticism can be handled effectively.

The Six Keys for Effectively Handling Criticism

It turns out that there are six keys to effectively handling criticism. First, you want to understand clearly *why* you have decided to deal more effectively with criticism, not just because criticism hurts but because it can easily deflect you from your path in life and prevent you from making the meaning you intend to make. Gaining this clear understanding is the *existential key*. Second, you want to be able to appraise situations in the blink of an eye, instantly taking their existential weight into account, so that you can consciously decide whether or not you are going to take any notice of what was just said or what just happened. This is the *appraisal key*.

Third, you want to acquire a certain cheerful, phlegmatic, philosophical attitude that allows you to dismiss most criticism effortlessly and let it simply evaporate. This is the *attitudinal key*. Fourth, you want to gain control of how your mind deals with the criticism that it deems it must address, mastering the art of bringing your self-talk in line with your intentions. This is the *cognitive key*.

Fifth, you want to be able to manage your own personality so that you respond to criticism in ways that do not weaken you, embroil you in unproductive dramas, or otherwise fail to serve you. This is the *personality key*. Sixth, you want to learn what sort of actions you can take to best deal with the sting of criticism, to prevent future criticism, and to make any changes that you deem necessary to make. This is the *behavioral key*.

Let's carefully examine these six keys, as each one is valuable in its own right. If you were to master just one of them, you would have helped yourself enormously in your quest to rid your life of toxic criticism. If you can master all six, you will dramatically decrease the amount and the toxicity of the criticism that comes your way.

The Existential Key

Until you decide that your path in life matters, that it is ultimately your responsibility to live by your cherished principles, and that you and only you can create a life worth living, you will have insufficient motivation to put criticism in its place. You will allow yourself to be bruised and battered by criticism simply because you don't have more important matters to consider.

If your goal is to paint and you decide that nothing will deflect you from that path because you know that painting is *the* place where you can make meaning, then when a friend or a loved one remarks that modern painting is silly or that painting is an elitist activity, you have no trouble dealing with that criticism. It goes in one ear and out the other because you have trumped all criticisms of that sort with your conviction that what you are doing makes sense to you and must be upheld with your whole being.

It turns out that to deal effectively with criticism, you need a solid sense of what matters in your life. Insofar as the meanings in your life are built on sand, you are vulnerable to wounding by what people say and do. If you half-doubt that painting is meaningful or suspect that your painting isn't up to snuff and probably never will be, you will leave yourself wide open to pain. Every time a person visits your studio and takes no interest in your work, every time someone waxes ironic about modern art, every time your mate lets slips that you are something of a leech for failing to bring in any income, you will feel hard-pressed not to let that criticism get under your skin. By virtue of doubting your path, you let the criticism in.

Can you not doubt something that you do in fact doubt? Wouldn't that amount to a charade or to denial? How can you act as if you know that painting is the right place to make meaning if you don't know that for a fact? How you answer this pivotal question will determine in large measure how well you handle the criticism in your life. If your answer is "Since I'm not sure, I'll proceed uncertainly and allow myself to be buffeted by every chance remark," you will have turned yourself into flypaper for criticism. If your answer is "Since I'm not sure, I'll proceed with fierce conviction and monitor my own thoughts on the matter," you will have made the best out of an existential dilemma and safeguarded yourself against idle criticism.

Whether you are certain about your path in life or uncertain about it, your best bet is to demand of yourself that you will remain the single most important arbiter of your existential reality and, as a corollary principle, that what others say *must* be taken with a grain of salt. This is not to say that you can't learn from other people, that other people might not sometimes point out important things that you've missed, or that you are invariably right and that the world is invariably muddled. What it means is that you will not abdicate your responsibility to make the meaning in your life. If and when you fully embrace that responsibility, you will change your relationship to the world and make yourself less vulnerable to toxic criticism.

The Appraisal Key

To make sense of your life and take charge of it, you need to get in the habit of quickly appraising situations rather than defensively reacting. This is the kind of instant appraisal required: You want to decide in the blink of an eye whether a comment is existentially worth bothering with—if it falls into a category that you deem meaningful. If it does, you next want to decide whether the comment is objectively true or objectively false. Next you want to decide, whether it is true or false, if it rises to a level of importance that makes it worth considering. In this way you train yourself to dismiss comments, whether true or false, that are not existentially important or that are existentially important but not *that* important.

Take the following scenario. You work from home. Your husband works at an office. Because you work from home, your business tends to sprawl throughout the house, creating a bit of a mess (maybe more than a bit!). This doesn't bother you; you straighten up on the weekend and all is well. But every weekday evening when your husband comes home, he exclaims, "What a mess!"

and then goes about his routine, checking the mail, changing his clothes, and so on.

Obviously that "What a mess!" is not a friendly greeting on the order of "I'm home, dear!" It is a criticism. But even though it is a criticism, it is worth addressing only if it *is* worth addressing. That is what you want to appraise. Your appraisal might take the following form and last not even a second: "My business is going beautifully and, yes, it does create a bit of a mess, but if I stop to straighten every day I will get infinitely less work done, so I have no intention of doing that. It would be nice if Jeff were less of a jerk and would stop making that 'What a mess!' comment every day, but I am not interested in fighting with Jeff, educating Jeff, or changing Jeff, so I choose to let him off the hook and me off the hook and act as if he sneezed rather than spoke."

This analysis takes a lot of words on the page but virtually no time in the mind. You decide that this is a matter of existential importance, connecting to both your work life and your relationship life, and that therefore you must consider it at least a little bit. You do consider it a little bit, and you decide that while it is "objectively fair" criticism in the sense that a mess does exist, it is unfair in several other senses—that this is your work space as well as your living space, that the mess does get tidied every weekend, and so on. Most important, you decide that it simply doesn't rise to the level of being worth considering. This complete appraisal, which takes microseconds or seconds at most, allows you to label Jeff's daily comment as nothing more than a grunt or a belch.

Of course, you may decide that Jeff's comment needs addressing. In that case, you would make use of the strategies we'll discuss as we proceed. When you appraise, you hold yourself ready for two possible outcomes, that the situation is of no concern to you and that dismissal and detachment are the keys or that the situation is of some moment and should be addressed. Insofar as you have made real sense of the first key and refuse to be deflected from your meaning-making path by idle comments, and real sense of the third key and adopt an attitude so sunny, phlegmatic, and philosophical that the world's darts do not find in you a dartboard, the more likely you will be to appraise most critical comments and situations as simply not worth your attention.

The Attitudinal Key

If you believe your attitude is not in your control, in whose control do you take it to be? Do you believe you *must* be pessimistic because you have reasons for being pessimistic? Do you take it that you *must* be depressed because so many things are going miserably? Do you believe you *must* keep a wary, critical eye on every aspect of your environment and your life because you were harmed as a child and felt unsafe and unloved? You might respond, "Well, I just don't have any reason to feel sunny, phlegmatic, and philosophical about life because life is s*#t," to which I must respond, "That's a mistake."

It turns out that a pessimistic, self-critical, world-wary, half-depressed, anxious, sorrowful, passive, or defeated attitude does not feel good and does not serve you, even if you can produce a ton of reasons why that is the logical attitude to adopt. Even if you can produce a mountain of evidence for why you should be gloomy, wary, and out of sorts, it doesn't follow that actually *being* gloomy, wary, and out of sorts is the way for you to be. You will have to decide two things: whether your attitude is in your control and what you want your attitude to be.

The attitude that will go the longest way toward inoculating you against toxic criticism starts with your believing in yourself, in your choices and your path, and in your ability to right your ship if it is off course. You believe in yourself and laughingly shrug off the opinions of others, not because you suppose others never have anything to say, but because you deeply understand to what extent everyone has an agenda and how often people are completely wrong in their opinions. If people knew what they were talking about, how could there be two hundred thousand different religions (the actual number that cultural anthropologists have identified)? Are you going to listen to *anyone* about the nature of the universe with all those people yammering that *they* know—and each making a different claim? Shouldn't you smile and shrug instead?

Smiling, shrugging, and keeping your own counsel will make a huge percentage of what previously felt like criticism evaporate. Smiling and shrugging when your mother says something about the lack of fish oil in your diet (which next week she will be recommending against, as her hairdresser happened upon an article contradicting last week's previous "latest findings") is the perfect approach and turns her opinions, which have always felt critical of you, into absurd, idle rants. When a coworker wants to "tell you something for your own good" and you smile, shrug, and say, "I'd love to hear what you have to say and maybe we can chat about it next Thursday," you retain control and your good humor. The keys: smiling, shrugging philosophically, and *keeping your own counsel.*

Adopting this attitude doesn't require that you genuinely believe in yourself, only that you intend to operate *as if* you genuinely believed in yourself. If you actually do believe in yourself, that is wonderful!—and rare. Your current levels of self-confidence, self-esteem, and self-trust, if they happen to be low, can't be allowed to prevent you from adopting an attitude that will serve you well. The more you train yourself not to allow the world to dictate to you, bring you down, or control your moods and opinions, the more you train yourself to find that reserve in you that is optimistic, life-loving, and hopeful. The more you decide to adopt an everyday attitude of wry amused pleasure, the better off you will be.

The Cognitive Key

Because you have come to understand your path and what is true for you, a certain large percentage of the criticism directed your way will never actually reach you, stopped in its tracks by the strength of your convictions. Because of your new phlegmatic, philosophical attitude and your ability to decide on the spot whether a given barb rises to the level of significance, virtually nothing infiltrates as criticism. But some comments and situations will rise to the level of significance and will require your attention.

At these times you want to gain control of how your mind works and master the art of bringing your self-talk into line with your intentions. Even if you deem certain criticism to be fair and telling, even if you are brought up short by a comment and suddenly have your eyes opened to big mistakes you've been making or real problems with your personality, you want to retain control of your self-talk. It is one thing to feel momentarily foolish, ashamed, despairing, and so on. It is another thing to let control of your mind slip away and turn a problem into a disaster.

The Buddha instructed, "Get a grip on your mind!" Eastern and Western psychologists, whether in the Buddhist tradition or the cognitive/behavioral tradition, have identified inappropriate self-talk as *the* cause of emotional suffering. The things we say to ourselves drive us and cause us to hate ourselves, hate others, give up, give in to our appetites, fail to reach our goals— and stand wide open to criticism. Indeed, the things we say to ourselves most often *are* criticisms. Virtually no one is as critical of us as we are.

What does it mean to "get a grip on your mind"? It means you are brave enough to notice what you say to yourself, savvy enough to identify which inner talk is harmful or counterproductive, strong enough to dispute that kind of self-talk, and resourceful enough to replace it with useful "thought substitutes." You hear yourself say, "I'm a real loser," instantly identify that as counterproductive self-talk, shake your fist at yourself, and replace "I'm a real loser" with "I'm going to give life a try." That, in a nutshell, is how you get a grip on your mind.

Say your boss confronts you with the fact that you've been late to work four days out of five. You accept that as both a fair criticism and one important enough not to ignore, since you like this job and want to keep it. Your next task, after deciding that this criticism must be reckoned with, is to get a grip on your mind and frame the matter correctly. To say internally, "I've screwed up and I'm going to lose my job" amounts to self-criticism and only serves to tarnish your self-esteem and scare you. To say, "He may be right, but he's such a jerk that I don't really care" amounts to defensive self-sabotage. To say, "I'm feeling sick, and I have to go home right now" is to allow your anxiety and embarrassment to govern your self-talk. These, and self-statements like them, are the unfortunate ways we respond to situations when we haven't trained ourselves to get a grip on our mind.

What is right thinking in this situation? It is bravely hearing yourself say, "He may be right, but he is such a jerk that I don't really care" and recognizing that defensively attacking your boss and feigning indifference aren't the thoughts that you want to be thinking. You dispute that response with every fiber of your being and substitute "I need to take a minute, breathe, and think about this" in place of the defensive thoughts your mind first produced.

Even better is not to think the inappropriate thought in the first place. Instead of continually having to dispute and change unproductive thinking, your ultimate goal is to think the right thought the first time. When your boss says, "Susan, you know you've been late four days this week, and that's not OK," you want to say to yourself (after you've appraised this as one of those situations that needs your attention and must be addressed), "That's true. What's been going on this week? I need to think about this." You do not attack yourself; you do not defend yourself; you do not flee the scene; you treat it as a moment that requires your authentic consideration and participation.

The Personality Key

Personality is both formed and fluid, static and dynamic. If the brain is the most complicated bit of matter in the universe, personality may amount to the most complicated set of dynamics in the universe. Sometimes you react reflexively; sometimes you stop yourself from acting reflexively and consider your reaction. Sometimes you operate from the shadows, leading with the dark side of your personality; sometimes you operate from the light. Sometimes you feel yourself to be nothing but a walking addiction, incapable of not overdoing the buffet; sometimes you operate in a principled and disciplined way for days on end.

As a rule, and unless you've put these keys into practice, when you are hit with a bit of toxic criticism you react reflexively, bringing forth the personality piece that you habitually bring forth when attacked. Maybe you mourn and drink. Maybe you get angry and dream of revenge. Maybe you get very small and hide for weeks. Maybe you try to deny that it happened and smile a false smile. Maybe you make very big changes in the blink of an eye, dropping a career, quitting a job, leaving a relationship, or splitting town. Most people react reflexively in the face of toxic criticism, just as they would react if they had touched a hot stove.

Consider the following scenario. A novelist devotes four years to writing a novel. During that time she also struggles to lose fifty pounds and to keep depression at bay. A literary agent reads her novel and informs her that it is an unmitigated disaster. Worse, the author recognizes that each of the agent's criticisms is fair and that the novel is unsalvageable. This is an existentially crucial criticism, one that connects directly to the way she has decided to make meaning in life and can't be met with a sunny attitude and a philosophical shrug. What is this author likely to do if she can't manage her reaction at the deep level of personality? She is likely to fall off her diet and balloon, sink into a severe depression, open herself up to opportunistic illness, and call herself the worst names imaginable.

This is the epitome of toxic criticism, criticism so virulent that it can destroy you by virtue of the way it undermines your sense of self and drains the meaning right out of your life. The criticism and self-criticism may be relatively more fair or unfair, as even an objectively wretched novel is still an accomplishment that could be celebrated, but whether it is more fair or unfair, it is experienced as a terrific blow. If this author reacts reflexively with pain, despair, an eating binge, and so on, this blow will amount to a true catastrophe. If, on the other hand, she can somehow manage her personality and her self-talk, she has the chance to survive this blow with minimal damage.

What would "managing her personality" amount to in this scenario? Nothing so simple as managing her self-talk and substituting more affirming language for the terrible language suddenly coursing her brain, though that is a vital part of the solution. In addition to employing the magic of self-cognitive therapy, she would want to calm herself so she could think clearly and mindfully examine her options, fervently recommit to her diet program, monitor her behaviors to make sure she hadn't started behaving from the shadows, monitor her mood and engage in activities that worked to minimize depression, and so on. Her working mantra might amount to something like the following:

"I am going to think the right thoughts *and* be the right me as I deal with this calamity."

The Behavioral Key

In the case of our novelist—let's call her Sarah—there are many real-world behaviors that she will want to engage in to help her recover from this blow and prevent these toxins from eating her alive. She will want to eat moderately and not binge, as putting weight back on will only compound her problems. She will want to stroll in the sun, as sunlight is a natural antidepressant. She will want to refrain from making any big changes in her life, as changes made during a crisis are often not the right ones. Most important, she will want to tackle her writing life in concrete, active ways.

She has several choices with respect to this novel. She can revise it. She can reread it to see if it really is as flawed as she now believes it to be. She can send it out to additional readers to gauge their opinion. She can carve it up into short stories and begin to circulate them. She can pay a freelance editor to edit it. She can have a conversation with herself about her intentions with respect to this novel and see if she can get clarity as to what went wrong (if, in fact, anything did).

If the novel can't be salvaged, she has to move on. She can think through whether another meaning-making avenue is open to her that will serve her as well as writing has served her and, if so, pursue meaning there. If she sees writing as the place where she wants to continue making meaning, then she will have to choose her next writing project (or let it choose her) and begin a new piece of writing. What she can't do is let this existential crisis fester unresolved. She must take action in the real world if the toxicity of this moment is to be released and overcome.

Whether the criticism we receive is more fair or unfair, life-altering or merely unpleasant, rooted deep in the past or completely of the moment, there will always be real-world actions we need to take to deal with the criticism. This is true because we intend to bring to bear the best parts of our personality to deal with the criticism, and that requires that we do actual things—like eat our vegetables rather than binge on chocolate, increase our twelve-step meetings rather than hurt ourselves, bravely leave the apartment rather than anxiously refusing to leave. A toxic episode, because it is bound to have repercussions on our system, must be dealt with actively—or else it is not really being dealt with at all.

These keys require mindfulness on your part. They also require that you master the emotional charge that attaches to criticism, since that flood of emotion is likely to ruin your chances of accurately appraising the situation, effectively managing your self-talk, and so on. What if you knew that you could deal with the emotion "later that day" and, as a consequence, defuse the charge and bring mindfulness to bear in the moment? That would prove a real godsend. You can do exactly that by learning the strategy of writing "Dear critic" letters, a strategy examined in the next chapter.

To consider

- What is your intuitive guess as to which of the six keys will be hardest for you to master?
- Do you have clarity as to what your meaning-making goals and life purposes are?
- Which of your methods for dealing with criticism do you consider effective, and which do you consider ineffective?

- In what ways would you like to react differently in the moment when someone criticizes you?

To do

- Reread the description of the six keys to handling toxic criticism and reframe them in your own language so that you begin to "own" them.
- Write down your thoughts about the six keys, focusing on challenges you foresee and how you will meet those challenges.
- Create a "life purpose statement" that articulates your meaning-making goals and life purposes (in conjunction with making sense of and mastering the existential key).

2

Employing "Dear Critic" Letters

You've just been criticized. You feel your face turning beet red. You want to defend yourself, but your brain has turned to mush. You want to hide, but you know that running out of the room will feel just too humiliating and will make you feel even worse than standing right where you are. What can you do to deal with the seething emotions that are making it impossible for you to think straight and deal adequately with the criticism?

You might have done many things to prepare yourself for this moment. We discussed six of them in the last chapter. You might have gotten so clear on your life purposes and your life path that your existential filter traps most criticism before it has a chance to do any damage. You might have gotten so practiced at appraising situations—especially at waving away those that are not important enough to consider—that you feel equal to handling criticism in a level-headed way. You might have adopted a phlegmatic, philosophical attitude that allows you to brush aside most criticism as commentary on the foibles of human nature and nothing that reflects on you. You might stand ready to deal with your self-talk and your personality and feel confident that you will take the appropriate action, should action be required of you. In short, you might have already transformed yourself into somebody better able to dismiss most criticism out of hand and better able to manage and process the remaining criticism.

You might have transformed yourself already. But even if you have, you will still want to possess tactics for dealing with that portion of toxic criticism that makes its way in and inflames your emotions. One tactic to deal with this remaining criticism is to acquire the habit of writing "Dear critic" letters. If you know that as soon as you get home you will be able to vent your feelings and process the toxic incident in private, you will feel more grounded, present, and powerful in the moment.

How "Dear Critic" Letters Can Help You

A "Dear critic" letter is a letter that you write but almost never send. In it, you address the person who has criticized you and let him or her know about the anger, displeasure, sadness, or other emotion that the criticism evoked; your sense of outrage, injustice, or betrayal; and your feelings about the unfairness of the criticism, if it seemed unfair, or about its delivery, if it seemed cruelly delivered. In your "Dear critic" letter you get everything off your chest. Your goal in this letter is, first and foremost, to *freely vent* and release the toxins that are circulating in your system.

It is excellent to *just vent*. Many people do not have permission to own their feelings. They feel angry but aren't comfortable being angry and look for ways not to feel angry by rationalizing away their feelings, self-medicating, denying that anything happened, and so on. Venting in public and laying into the person who criticized you can have serious negative consequences; but those negative consequences do not attach to a letter you write and do not mail. Writing a "Dear critic" letter is the equivalent of pounding your fists, screaming, or engaging in some other delicious venting activity. Here is a short, sweet "Dear critic" letter written by a young woman named Theresa.

Dear Negative Know-It-All,

I bet it seemed so easy for you. Just say anything you damn well please! It was just an offhanded comment you made, and I bet you already don't remember it, though it was just this afternoon. Well, I remember it! Words can hurt, and the hurt can run very deep. So what if you think I'll never make it as a writer? What do you know? There was absolutely no reason for you to tell me I should stop trying! It's been only a few hours, but I'm already tired of carrying this hurt and anger around. You had no right to talk to me like that! You had no right to put me down just so you could feel a little better! This may even be good-bye—and if it is, I can't say that I am going to miss you!

Not your whipping girl,
Theresa

"Dear critic" letters allow you to vent. They serve a second purpose that is even more important. They allow you to process the incident and begin to own your part of the criticism. You express your feelings, but you also appraise accurately and mete out responsibility fairly. In the following "Dear critic" letter a young painter apportions blame while venting her feelings about one of her painting instructors:

Dear Mr. Jones,

I am writing to object to your scathing final criticism of my semester of painting. First of all, I know I wasn't working to my potential. I was going through all sorts of personal issues, from my parents' impending divorce to my own drinking and drug problems. I'll take responsibility for that. However, you had no right to tear apart my work the way you did. I left feeling that I could never take another painting class again (and I just realized that I haven't!), that I'd never be a good enough painter, and that I should be ashamed of my very existence.

I fought hard to avoid bursting into tears, as I had too much pride to let you see my emotional response. But afterward I was so depressed that I don't even remember what I did next. Probably I went to the student union and drank beers or found a friend and smoked some pot. Yes, I wasn't together. But still I didn't deserve your scathing "review," even if I sometimes failed to show up for class or even if I failed to complete much of my work.

I've been punishing myself for my part in all of that, and I need to stop. I hope that writing this will help put both our parts of that disaster into perspective so that I can begin to heal. I wish I'd chosen a better instructor; I wish I hadn't let my anguish, fear, and low self-esteem prevent me from painting; and I truly wish you could have been more of a human being. Now I need to put this where it belongs: in the past.

Sincerely,
Tabitha

Clarifying Choices

A "Dear critic" letter addresses your critic and gives him or her a piece of your mind. It also allows you to enter into dialogue with yourself, identify your own personality challenges, and grow, heal, and change. It can serve a third purpose as well, that of helping you clarify your life choices and career path and make better sense of the existential issues that confront you.

You might learn as you write your "Dear critic" letter that it is time to take a big risk and start a home business, move from the rural quiet of your current life to the hubbub of a city for the sake of your career, or jettison your current church as you work through your crisis of faith. Here is a "Dear critic" letter that a client of mine, a well-known screenwriter—let's call him Eddie—found himself writing, both to vent at a certain director and to clarify his options to himself:

Dear Director X,

I've watched you "develop" my script for two years, a process that involved removing me from the creative dialogue, replacing me with writers who had no affinity for my work, and reshaping the work to fit your own vision. In the process, despite your assurance that you would protect the themes and meaning of the work, you gutted my smart social satire and replaced it with an unrecognizable and grotesquely crass sex comedy. Despite that, you have the gall to insist to me that this is the "best" version of the script. Well, sir, that just isn't true.

Now I'm left with an excruciating choice. I can allow you to reoption the material and proceed with your crass sex comedy. This has certain financial rewards for me—it will certainly enable me to write for a long time with some money in the bank. However, if I do that, I'll have to endure seeing my best work to date reduced to something ugly. In addition, I'll probably be unable to take my name off it, and I'll always be associated with the product of your misguided tampering. Of course, I can withdraw the script from the market, but the downside of that is, because of the costs accrued against this script, withdrawing it will ensure that it will never get made.

I guess the biggest disappointment in this whole mess is that you convinced me that you were respectful of my work, when in fact you weren't. I really had no idea how arrogant, shortsighted, and two-faced you were. But I will say this—lately integrity has become the central focus of my life. How does it feel to do the right thing instead of the expedient or the desperate thing? Well, Mr. X, it feels really good. I am delighted to fight for what I believe is right, whatever the results. I will take that feeling of integrity away from this process, whatever I choose to do next. At best, you will take away a bad movie.

Sincerely,
Eddie Smith

A careful reader will recognize that Eddie wrote this letter not in response to any criticism of him or his work but because of a *toxic situation* about which *he* was feeling critical. This is our first taste of the following theme, that you will regularly find yourself in a position where *you* are the one feeling critical or the one offering up the criticism. You may have to criticize ("evaluate") an employee at work, criticize ("advise") your best friend, criticize ("educate") your students, and so on. Whatever euphemism you use for what you are doing and however fine your intentions, whenever you have to tell someone something that is in any way critical, you become the critic. In situations like that, you can use a "Dear critic" letter of the sort that Eddie wrote to prepare yourself to say carefully what you deem needs saying.

Healing from the Past

Until criticism from the past can be released, it keeps circulating in our system, making us anxious, causing depressions, and undermining our resolve. You can use the "Dear critic" letter-writing process to help release those old hurts. Here are two examples, one (from Laura) where the critic was a family member, the second (from Samantha) where the critic was a teacher.

Dear Dad,

I'm sorry you feel the B+ I got on my report card wasn't good enough. Does that mean I'm not good enough? I think that's how you feel. But people aren't perfect, and I'm no exception. I understand that you didn't reach the level of education and standard of living you wanted, but that doesn't make you a failure any more than getting a B+ makes me a failure. Can't you see that?

I can't go on feeling like I'm not as good as other people, that I'm flawed and worthless. I live in fear of being judged by everyone, so I don't take chances, I don't put myself out there for fear of looking stupid and wrong. I judge myself that way! I know you want people to see us (our family, you, Mom) as better than we are, but no one is better than anyone else, just different. I wish I could show you that you are as good as you need to be—as good as anyone else.

Since you are alive now only in my memory, it's my responsibility to stop criticizing and judging myself. It is my job to convince the part of me that comes from your need to make me perfect, that I am as good as anyone else, as good as I need to be. It's OK not to be the best at everything; it's even OK not to be the best in my strongest areas. An interesting insight I'm having right now is that I'm not even sure what my strongest areas are because I have not allowed myself to really try anything. So I feel pretty mediocre at everything—and I don't even have permission to show that mediocrity. That has got to end, Dad!

I love you, Dad, and I miss you,
Laura

In this second example Samantha makes peace with her demeaning parochial school experience, epitomized by one nun in particular.

Dear Sister Maria,

You have hung around long enough in my head, and it is time for you to GOOOOO. You had no right to say those things to me when I was in your class as a junior. People have potential. They evolve, expand, learn from their mistakes, develop new understanding. You honored none of that. How dare you close the door on something that was so important to me, my writing, something that has only become more important over time! How could you make such high-and-mighty pronouncements to someone so young, with all of life's possibilities still open to her?

Teachers like you need to be kept far away from children! I despise you for your poor attitude and for the outsized influence you had on my life. I know you are part of the reason I had such a struggle with my writing, particularly as a young adult. You were supposed to offer CONSTRUCTIVE suggestions, damn it! But you were just mean, cruel, and nasty. I give you an F.

Good-bye, eleventh-grade creative writing class!
Samantha

Lessening Anxiety Over Anticipated Criticism

You can also use this letter-writing process to deal with criticism that hasn't occurred yet—that is, to deal with *anticipated criticism*. Many people are hampered from following their dreams because they fear the criticism they are likely to receive or, in many cases, bound to receive were they to live their dream. For many people, anticipated criticism is even more toxic than any actual criticism they have ever received.

You can't choose to be a writer and also hope to avoid criticism. You can't choose to be a painter and also hope to avoid criticism. You can't choose to advocate a controversial issue and also hope to avoid criticism. You can't do anything with a public face and in a personal voice and also hope to avoid criticism. People intuitively know this and know they have two choices, to deal with the criticism when it comes or to refuse even to try. Many choose the latter path.

You can use the "Dear critic" letter-writing process to reduce your fear and anxiety about future criticism, to learn precisely how you want to deal with your future critics, and to train yourself to dismiss most of that future criticism out of hand. You can disempower your future critics and empower yourself by giving them a piece of your mind right now and letting them know you will not allow them to creep into your head and prevent you from living your life.

Here are two examples of "Dear critic" letters of this sort, the first from Leslie to her imaginary critic.

Dear Imaginary Someone,

I do not thank you for your criticism of me and my singing and playing. I was extremely upset and hurt by your implicit rejection, by your snickers behind my back, by your looking down your nose at me, by your calling me an inferior musician with your eyes. I do not thank you for calling my show a disaster, for calling me an amateur, and for not inviting me to participate in the next show you're putting together. I do not thank you for any of that.

I do not thank you for encouraging my desire to give up this business altogether, for making me feel even more justified in holing myself up in my room and not practicing what I most need to learn. The vision of your face makes acid rise up in the back of my throat. I do not like feeling judged by you. I do not like it that you increase my dread and even make me afraid to go outside. I hate the idea that we will come face-to-face one day and I will be the one running from your line of sight. Well, I won't! I do not thank you, but I know we are going to meet. I swear I am not going to run away from you!

Leslie

The second example comes from a doctoral student stymied on her dissertation by the constant worry that experts in her field were bound to criticize her ideas.

Dear expert in all that I would like to be an expert in—gender theory, symbolic anthropology, women's health, and adolescent health—

who writes perfect essays and has read all of Foucault and Proust in French:

Instead of focusing on my dissertation and just doing the work, I let you, expert in all things important, fill up my mind. You loom up and say "that part is terrible, throw it out, cut it up, it is useless," or "there is no logical thread running through the text, it makes no sense, you have no idea what you are doing." You bash my writing, you make me dislike my text . . . well, almost, but not quite.

Not quite. Here I return to my personal responsibility toward the work. Do I want to let someone else tell me what I can and cannot do? Do I want to fear what you will say in some distant, imaginary future? Can I live with the idea that I am not capable of mastering my material? It will not be easy to sit down to an imperfect version of my dissertation, and it will not be easy to actually do the work. Ah, well! Maybe I will meet you one day, and maybe you will be right in all your criticisms. Today, I must just work.

Elizabeth

Silencing Your "Inner Critic"

In addition to using the "Dear critic" letter-writing process to defuse the sting of criticism received today, criticism received decades ago, or criticism you fear will come in the future, you can use the process to begin to deal with self-criticism and your own "inner critic." You personify your inner critic and give it a good piece of your mind. In essence, you have an important chat with yourself (as Leandra does in this example) about the whys of your own self-bashing and announce that you intend to stop it.

Dear little shitty voice inside my head,

Why do you constantly put me down and tell me that my art "isn't good enough"?! Why must you constantly torment me? You think you're terribly clever, but I have news for you. I'm going to beat you! I don't know when, and I don't know how, but I know I will. Art is not something I want to create; it is something I am called to create. I deny myself and my god when I listen to you. So why do I do it? I haven't figured out that answer yet, but when I do, you better watch out!

Maybe I'll always have to hear you. I hope not, but maybe you're too damned devilishly clever. Then I just won't listen. I'll become so strong and sure of myself that all of your nagging complaints about how bad I am will just fall on deaf ears. I will win! I haven't the slightest doubt that you are terribly powerful, terribly subversive, terribly clever. You know all the things to say, since you are right there inside me, watching me react and falter. Yes, you have a great vantage point and a great advantage! But I am going to win because I am staking my life on it.

Leandra

Very often a bout of self-criticism is provoked by a piece of criticism hurled our way. Mom says we lack self-discipline, and that activates the voice inside our head that agrees that we lack self-discipline. The boss makes a face as he reads the manual we've written, and that prompts us to criticize ourselves for never having properly learned grammar. You can use the "Dear critic" letter-writing process to deal simultaneously with external and internal criticism, as Patricia did in the following letter.

Dear bow-tied critic and my own inner gremlins,

When I was asked to play the cello at the opening of that exhibition of paintings, I intended to play some easy Celtic tunes and evergreens and not impress any "real musicians" who might happen to be in the audience. When you glared at me and said: "You really should practice your cello more, madam," I felt stunned. Instantly my own gremlins, the ones that know I hardly ever practice, started chiming in. I already have feelings of inferiority because I have a problem with practicing and because I haven't been to a conservatory.

You are obviously discerning when it comes to cello playing. You correctly saw the inadequacies in my playing. It irritates me that yours is the comment I remember, not all the compliments I got, and not the fact that a theater director offered me a job on the strength of my playing. You were right, but wasn't the theater director also right? Gremlins! Didn't the compliments also count?

I think you were probably a classical musician and knew how hard professionally trained people have to work. It may have raised your ire that someone who hasn't had professional training was playing a classical instrument in public and being paid for it—what a nerve! Well, I do have nerve. I give people pleasure, and I am musical. Writing this letter has made me see that I must accept myself as I am, even the fact that I am a part-time musician who doesn't practice enough. Part of my strength and power resides in the fact that I can pick up my cello, enjoy it, and please (nonfastidious) people. Yes, gremlins, you are still running around my head, tormenting me. But my ambition is to ignore you and bow-tied critics alike.

Yours sincerely,
Patricia

I think you're beginning to get a sense of what I'm proposing: that you transform yourself into a person who stands in a different, better relationship to criticism and that you acquire an arsenal of tactics and strategies that help you deal with the criticism that comes your way. You want to be *transformed* and *armed*. The six keys discussed in Chapter 1, if followed, amount to a transformational program. The strategy introduced in this chapter, of writing strategic "Dear critic" letters, and the strategies and tactics discussed in the next two chapters will fill up your toolbox with the right resources for handling toxic barbs aimed your way.

To consider

- Do you believe there is power and utility in venting, or do you see venting as dangerous, self-indulgent, or inappropriate?
- Do you currently have a way of chatting with yourself on paper about the issues that are "up" in your life? If you do, do you see writing "Dear critic" letters as a useful tool?
- Can you see yourself getting in the habit of writing "Dear critic" letters? If not, why not?

To do

- Write a "Dear critic" letter in response to a recent critical incident or event.
- Write a "Dear critic" letter that helps heal the past.
- Write a "Dear critic" letter that helps inoculate you against future anticipated criticism.
- Write a "Dear critic" letter to yourself, to deal with some aspect of your self-critical nature.
- Write a letter in which you work through your own critical feelings about someone (as Eddie did in his letter to Director X).

3

Putting the Six Keys into Practice: Tasks and Tactics

In the last chapter I presented one specific tactic—writing "Dear critic" letters—that helps you ventilate your feelings and understand your situation. However, each of the six keys from Chapter 1 can be broken down further into constituent parts, and tactics and strategies are available for each constituent part. In this chapter we look at tasks associated with managing toxic criticism and the concrete tactics and strategies you can employ to transform yourself into someone less willing and less likely to be criticized.

Don't expect to be able to use these many tactics and strategies in a consistent or linear way. Virtually no one can adopt the totality of a transformational program. Your better bet is to read through this chapter and then set aside a little time to decide which of these tactics you want to incorporate into your life. Even if you choose to practice only a few of them, you will be much better prepared to handle the toxic criticism that comes your way.

The Existential Key: Tasks and Tactics

The first key is the existential key: you prepare yourself to deal effectively with criticism by championing your own meaning-making efforts as a principled person pursuing certain life goals. Focused as you are on your meaning-making efforts, you suddenly find it easy to ignore most criticism as irrelevant. You are too busy making meaning to notice or bother with the world's barbs and arrows. In conjunction with this key, you have five tasks to tackle.

Task: What It Means to Decide to Matter

Do you matter to yourself? Are you firmly committed to living a principled, powerful, accomplished life? Until you can answer yes to these questions and until you live a life that reflects your affirmative choice to matter, your very existential unsettledness makes you an easy target for criticism. When people criticize you, you will be inclined to agree with them because you yourself feel critical of your lack of direction, motivation, and discipline. This transformational task of living as if you matter is central to your growth.

Tactic: Affirm That You Matter

Say, "What I do matters." "My life matters to me." "I amount to something." "I have a voice." Literally say these powerful, affirmative things and others like them. Say them out loud. Say them to the people in your life. Say to your mother, who routinely criticizes you, "Mother, I matter." Practice mattering.

Task: How to Feel You Are on a Personal Path

How are you conceptualizing your journey through life? Most people have no path in mind and operate reactively and reflexively, making it through the day at work, disliking their job but seeing no alternatives, feeling more tossed and turned by life than confidently at the helm. If you currently have no path in mind, how can you know which criticism to address and which to ignore? If someone criticizes you at work and you don't even know whether your job is important to you, how will you know how seriously to take the criticism? To put criticism in its place, you need to know what you are intending to do with your life.

Tactic: Map Your Path

To map your path, follow these three steps:

1. First, name the primary way you intend to make meaning: "I intend to be a writer."
2. Then articulate the details of that meaning-making path: "I intend to write novels, have them published, have a career as a novelist, and grow masterful as a writer."
3. Next, articulate your plan: "I will work at anything for the next three years as I write my first two novels, as I expect the first one to stink and the second one to be much better."

With this sort of mental map in mind, when your boss at your day job criticizes you for your lack of motivation, you can make a strategic reply while internally acknowledging the truth—and unimportance—of his criticism.

Task: Put Criticism in Its Place (in the Context of Existential Decisions)

Once you have a sense of your meaning-making path, you can begin to decide what sorts of criticisms are going to count and what sorts of criticisms you are going to ignore out of hand. If you decide your meaning-making path is writing, you can shrug off criticism of your singing voice and your snoring as minor and worth considering only insofar as you don't want to bring down your choir or keep up your lover. That is, you process criticism of this irrelevant sort to see what it means and what it implies, but you do so without any emotional charge attached because it does not connect to your meaning-making path.

Tactic: Ask Yourself, "Does This Criticism Connect to My Path?"

Memorize the question "Does this criticism connect to my path?" and learn to quickly remove the emotional sting from criticism that has no bearing on your authentic journey. When someone says, "You look tired today" or "You look like you've slept in your clothes," you instantly ask yourself, "Does this criticism connect to my path?" If you judge that it doesn't (for instance, because you look tired and like you've slept in your clothes *exactly because* you were up all night writing), you can dismiss it instantly with a smile and a "Yes, exactly."

Task: How to Deal with Meaning Drains and Meaning Crises

A given piece of criticism may relate to your path and deal you both an emotional and an existential blow. For instance, you might receive a rejection letter from an editor that reads in part, "This is so bad that I can't believe you had the gall to send it to me." Because this criticism relates directly to your meaning-making path, it hurts tremendously (while also providing potentially important information). You will need to vent the emotional hurt; but you will also need to deal with the meaning crisis that this rejection provokes.

Tactic: Visualize Meaning Returning

When you take an existential body blow and meaning drains out of your life, you immediately want to picture meaning returning and instantly say to yourself, "I know that I can make meaning again." A writer who receives a devastating critique needs to opt for hope rather than despair, picture his life buoyed up by meaning like some great ocean liner rising in dry dock as water rushes in. He needs to exclaim, "I know that my writing will feel meaningful again—and soon!"

Task: Relish Criticism as a Natural Consequence of Setting Goals and Taking Risks

You commit to make meaning *in* your life and *with* your life. As a consequence, you set goals and accept risks. You take on the role of warrior and announce that you will stake your life for your principles and your meaning-making ideals. Armored by your convictions, you ignore as harmless and irrelevant most criticism flung your way and even relish that criticism, as proof that you are fully in the fray. Because you are existentially solid, criticisms that others would find mortally wounding you experience as pinpricks.

Tactic: Announce That You Relish and Invite Criticism

Actually say, "I relish criticism!" Elaborate on that idea by exclaiming, "Criticize me all you like! I have bigger fish to fry!" Get in the habit of smiling at your critics. When someone criticizes you, laugh, shake your head, and stand a little taller. Feel like an action hero who must shoo away battalions of flies as you save the world. Feel like a heroic meaning maker and relish criticism as proof that you are stirring up the pot.

By affirming that you matter, mapping your meaning-making path, putting criticism in existential context, visualizing meaning returning after body blows, and relishing the criticism you receive as proof that you are really living, you will transform yourself into someone who is essentially unafraid of criticism. When someone criticizes you for having a messy apartment or feels obliged to inform you that you are sporting a few new wrinkles, you laugh those criticisms away as having absolutely no existential relevance. When a criticism does have some existential relevance, you stand resolute—a meaning-making warrior—and deal with the wound by dressing it with hope.

The Appraisal Key: Tasks and Tactics

Whether the criticism you receive is expected, like a work evaluation you are dreading, or completely unexpected, say from a stranger on the street, you want to be able to make certain decisions instantly. You can make these instant decisions only if you have trained yourself to *appraise* such situations rather than *react* to them reflexively and defensively. You do not want your doctor to react in horror at the sight of your wound, but rather you want him to know how to stop the bleeding. Similarly, you do not want to react emotionally when criticism hits; you want to understand what is going on and consciously decide how you intend to respond. In conjunction with this appraisal key, you have four tasks to master.

Task: How to Make Quick Sense of a Toxic Moment

Speed is of the essence in handling toxic criticism. You can always handle the criticism later, after the incident and in perfect solitude, but by opting to handle it later rather than on the spot you unnecessarily carry around toxins and lose the opportunity to dismiss criticism out of hand.

Tactic: Quickly Ask and Answer Five Questions

Appraising in the moment means learning to quickly ask and answer the following five questions:

1. **Have I actually been criticized?** You've just registered some comment as criticism. But is it really criticism? Is coming in third out of five hundred entries in a painting competition criticism or validation? You may be disappointed, irritated, even angry, but have you been *criticized*? Could it be that you are turning the moment into a toxic criticism moment when there is no good reason to do so? If the moment can be reframed better as something other than criticism, do that!

2. **What is the content of the criticism?** If your mother just criticized your haircut, is she criticizing your haircut, the fact that you are still single, or the fact that her hair hasn't looked good in thirty years? Or is it part of a bigger control issue? What is really going on? Attacking you because you are single and attacking you because she hates her hair are two very different things and should provoke very different responses in you.

3. **Is it fair or unfair criticism?** A neighbor comes into your apartment and exclaims, "Oh, how messy!" Because you are existentially and attitudinally armored, you dismiss her comment as her bile erupting and nothing with which you need concern yourself. But apart from the comment being rude and inappropriate, is it actually a true or false statement? No doubt your apartment is messier than apartments in advertisements. Is that the standard? No doubt it is messier than the apartment of a person with no life to lead who cleans all day long. Is that the standard? Is it so messy that rats have arrived? Probably your true appraisal will be "It is sort of average messy, and who cares?" That is, you will decide the criticism is not only unwarranted but objectively

unfair. Apply human-sized standards and quickly decide whether the criticism shot your way is fair or unfair.

4. **Whether it is fair or unfair, do I care?** You may agree that your apartment is messier than the average apartment, agree even that this reflects a problem that needs addressing, and still conclude that although it is a fair criticism and even a somewhat telling criticism, it is still so minor a matter that you simply do not care to give it a moment's thought. One of the most crucial appraisal tasks is deciding whether or not you want to *care* and, by caring, dignify this piece of criticism with your time and attention. Sometimes you will; but many, many times you won't.

5. **How do I want to respond?** Your final decision is whether to dismiss the criticism with a smile and a wave, make some other sort of response in the moment, or think the matter through and respond later. When you get practiced at responding effectively in the moment, the percentage of times that you respond on the spot will naturally increase. But as a rule you will probably find it wise to consider your response before delivering it—as many times you will decide against responding at all.

Task: Accurately Assessing What Troubles You Most About a Piece of Criticism

One of the most difficult aspects of dealing with toxic criticism is that, because of anxiety and defensiveness, we tend to do a very poor job of identifying what is actually bothering us about a piece of criticism. When your mother criticizes you, are you upset about the criticism, about the fact that her criticism makes you think she doesn't love you very much, or about the fact that you are so much like her that you want to scream? It takes courage, self-awareness, and fortitude to look a critical comment in the eye and accurately judge why it hurts so much.

Tactic: Ask, "What Is Actually Bothering Me?"

As a vital part of the appraisal process you want to ask yourself the brave question "What is actually bothering me?" about the criticism you receive. When your father criticizes you, your first thought might be "I hate him!" and you might naturally suppose that what is bothering you is his cruelty. But it may be the case that what is bothering you is that he is telling you a hard truth you don't want to hear. You can see why asking this vital appraisal question requires so much courage: by asking it, you are demanding of yourself that you own your part of the criticism, a part that may be substantial.

Task: Learning to Separate the Criticism from the Critic

Because a given piece of criticism may hurt but may also be fair and in our best interests, and because, even if it is unfair and cruel, it may still be delivered by someone with whom we need to maintain a decent relationship, it is wise to separate the criticism from the critic and not react defensively and angrily in the moment. The way to do this is to remain neutral and judicious, even when we are hurt and steaming.

Tactic: Internally Say, "I Am Not Going to Burn a Bridge Here"

Make the conscious decision that you are not going to respond in an inflammatory manner to criticism. Get in the habit of murmuring "I am not going to burn a bridge here" the instant you receive a critical blow. Occasionally this will mean missing an opportunity to vent appropriately, but over the long haul you will do yourself a world of good by responding calmly and carefully to the criticism that comes your way.

Task: Retaining Your Strength as You Appraise

You have just been hurt by a piece of toxic criticism. One natural reaction is to react angrily and defensively, as just discussed, and another reaction is to want to curl up in a ball and die. Because the latter is such a natural reaction, and because it produces weakness throughout our system, we want to consciously demand of ourselves that we remain strong in the moment. If we remain strong in the moment, we can more accurately appraise the situation and act more forcefully should the moment demand action.

Tactic: Possess a Warrior Practice

Martial artists practice. Fencers practice. Soldiers practice. They practice certain skills, but more important, they practice dealing with their fears and mastering their emotions. What sort of warrior practice makes sense for you? It might be tai chi, which is a peaceful adaptation of a warrior practice; it might be a sitting meditation practice, where the regimen of sitting strengthens your will as it cleanses your mind; or it might be some practice that you devise for yourself. Whether or not you actually practice, your goal is to *remember* to bring your warrior energy into the moment, not for the sake of fighting but for the sake of manifesting your natural strength.

The Attitudinal Key: Tasks and Tactics

Your attitude helps determine not only how you react to criticism but also how much you concern yourself with the criticism you receive. If you move through life anxious and vigilant, attuned to the opinions of others, and lacking necessary confidence, every little critical remark will register, strike you as toxic, and cause you emotional pain. If, on the other hand, you move through life with a philosophical perspective, a phlegmatic attitude, and the grace and strength of a peaceful warrior, few critical remarks will possess the power to harm you. In conjunction with this attitudinal key, you have five tasks to master.

Task: Growing Philosophical

If you opt to view the human animal with wry amusement, acknowledge the foibles of human nature, accept the universe as mysterious and ineffable, and cast a skeptical eye on the motives and methods of your fellow mortals, you will have adopted a philosophical attitude that allows you to put the essential unimportance of criticism in its place. By being philosophical about life and human nature, you instantly defang most criticism.

Tactic: Read the Philosophers

If you decide that it makes sense to adjust your attitude in a more philosophical direction, you may also conclude that it makes sense to tap into the wisdom of the philosophers. For example, you may read the writings of the great Stoics Epictetus, Cicero, Seneca, and Marcus Aurelius—each of whom had a lot to say about dignity and restraint. While it can be daunting to venture into a vast foreign territory like ancient philosophy, you may find the venture—and the adventure—worthwhile.

Task: Growing Phlegmatic

Growing philosophical involves orienting your mind in a certain direction, toward "not sweating the small stuff" and putting life's small challenges in wise perspective. Growing phlegmatic—growing calm, unemotional, and undemonstrative—involves orienting your personality in a similar direction. You present a stoic demeanor to the world, you train yourself not to be perturbed by other people's nonsense, and you decide beforehand that you are going to let very little ruffle your feathers. You ratchet down the intensity of interactions—rather than angling for drama—listen more than you speak, and present an impassive face to the hysterics of modern life.

Ancient wisdom had it that a phlegmatic personality signaled an individual keen on self-protection—and that is exactly right. You are *adopting* this personality style because it serves you as you pursue your meaning-making goals, not because it is the sunniest or warmest personality available to you. Be warm and sunny whenever you like—but have a phlegmatic overcoat available when the criticism starts flying.

Tactic: Practice Calmness

Phlegmatic people pride themselves on their calmness, a calmness that may come naturally or may be a studied habit. Whether calmness comes naturally to you or needs to be learned, it is an essential ingredient of the attitude change I'm suggesting. You learn to become calmer by practicing deep breathing techniques, mind-quieting meditation techniques, relaxation techniques, and other techniques that for millennia have proven to quell anxiety and produce calm.

Task: Learning Selective Inattention

Paying too much attention to every speck of dust and every critical remark are hallmarks of an anxious, vigilant person who is vulnerable to toxic criticism. Although you don't want to wander through life with your eyes closed, you do want to cultivate the habit of not noticing what you don't need to notice. You can select what you choose to notice and what you choose to ignore, from how much world news you let into your life to how much attention you pay to the antics of your coworkers. The better you focus on your meaning-making goals and filter out irrelevant data, including irrelevant insults and criticisms, the more you will feel truly on your own path.

Tactic: Practice Not Noticing

What do you notice when you get home from work? The dishes piled high in the sink (followed by a stab of self-criticism)? The bills piled high on the floor in front of the mail slot (followed by a stab of anxiety)? Practice not noticing these and the other bothersome things that routinely grab your attention the instant you step through the door. Instead, fix your attention where you would like to fix it: on your son, on the novel you sometimes write in the evening, or on the music you intend to listen to while you bathe. Take charge of where you focus your attention.

Task: Minding Your Own Counsel

When you see yourself as your own best friend and advocate and as the sole arbiter of what matters, you reduce the power of others to affect you with their opinions and criticism. You adopt the attitude that nothing anyone says is true or accurate until you have had a chance to weigh it against what you know to be true and accurate. If, for instance, someone says that an action of yours is immoral, you do not bat an eyelash and you do not accept even for an instant that he or she is right, no matter what arguments are adduced to prove you are bad. Instead, you listen and decide what *you* believe. If you let others call the shots about what constitutes right and wrong, you have turned yourself into a range target.

Tactic: Internally Ask, "What Do I Think?" in Response to Every Criticism

When you are criticized, your first task is to appraise the situation, as discussed earlier. What you are actually doing when you stop to appraise is deciding what you think about the situation. Rather than instantly believing the criticism and feeling hurt, you hold off feeling anything until you ask and answer the question "What do I think?" Just knowing that you are going to ask yourself this question provides a buffer between the criticism and a reflexive response. The next time you find yourself criticized, instead of reacting *at all*, step back and ask yourself, "What do I think?"

Task: Growing Graceful

The strong, calm, imperturbable, philosophical attitude that I suggest you cultivate amounts to a graceful way of being in the world, a way characterized by quiet self-assurance, wry, self-deprecating humor, and fierce convictions. People will recognize what this graceful way implies about your inner strength and will criticize you less often, as they will intuitively understand that you are not someone with whom they should trifle.

Tactic: Visualizing a Graceful You

Visualization is the practice of using your imagination as a self-help tool. You might visualize a calm scene so as to reduce your performance anxiety, visualize your healthy cells fighting your cancer cells so as to heal yourself from cancer, or, as in this case, visualize yourself gracefully handling criticism. By visualizing yourself gracefully handling criticism, you rehearse your new attitude and your new behaviors and get a picture in your mind of how you want to be.

The Cognitive Key: Tasks and Tactics

If the boss says, "The group has fallen behind today," one individual will take that as personal criticism and another individual will have no idea who or what is being criticized, as the boss hasn't been explicit yet. The second person has the healthier cognitive style: he or she isn't leaping to feeling criticized. This is an example of one of our cognitive tasks, changing our internal self-talk so as to reduce the number of times we actually experience criticism.

Let's say, however, that the boss is quite explicit and says, "Bill, you've fallen behind today." Another of our tasks is to carefully moderate our self-talk so that we don't turn this small criticism into a full-blown toxic event. These two tasks and three related ones constitute our work with respect to the cognitive key.

Task: Finding New Internal Language for Thinking About Criticism

Until we label something, the thing just is. We make a small mistake as we passionately play a piano concerto: one pianist will be mercilessly self-critical, and another pianist will think, "How beautifully I just played, that small flub notwithstanding!" You and you alone get to choose what language you employ in life, and you should consider that a blessing. It is a real blessing that you can eliminate an enormous percentage of the criticism in your life simply by training yourself not to call yourself into question so often. Does that amount to deluding yourself or letting yourself off the hook? Sometimes it may. But in general it is healthier to give yourself the benefit of the doubt than to demean and chastise yourself for your every move.

Tactic: Always Begin with "I Doubt I'm Being Criticized"

Your boss makes a face at you. Train yourself to think, "I doubt I'm being criticized" rather than "What did I do?" or "Is my job on the line?" or "The heck with him!" You receive a rejection form letter from an editor that reads in part, "Your material is not quite right for our publication." Train yourself to think, "I doubt I'm being criticized" rather than "She hates my writing," "I'm an idiot to think I can get published," or "Who the heck does she think she is?" By training yourself to react to potential criticism by thinking, "I doubt I'm being criticized," you will build up a reservoir of good feelings about yourself and allow yourself to process information (like the fact that your group is falling behind or an editor has passed on your story) without emotional turmoil.

Task: Modulating and Moderating Criticism

When we decide we should construe something as criticism and further decide we can't just slough the remark off but must think it through, our next job is to modulate and moderate how we talk to ourselves about the criticism in question. We do not want to feel that something catastrophic just happened, that we are ruined, that our life is suddenly bereft of meaning; we avoid these outsize feelings by carefully choosing the internal language we employ. Instead of saying, "My boss hates me and is sure to fire me," we say, "I fell a little behind today. I wonder what happened?"

Instead of saying, "I feel like a complete fool for missing so many notes in today's performance," we say, "That was an excellent performance, but I did miss a few notes. Should I be worried?" The language we use creates the feelings we feel. The more modulated our language, the less pain we inflict on ourselves.

Tactic: Say, "This Is No Big Deal"

When you decide that a certain piece of criticism needs to be considered, begin your considerations by defusing the situation and internally saying, "This is no big deal." For example: "It's no big deal that I got another rejection on my short story, but I do think I'd better consider what I want to do next. Do I need to polish the story one more time, send it out to different markets, or what?" By defusing the situation, rather than inflaming it, you manufacture less pain and allow yourself to think clearly.

Task: Learning New Methods for Controlling Self-Talk

It is an important first step to become aware of your self-talk and notice exactly what you are saying to yourself. Next, you need some methods for controlling your self-talk and moving it in the desired direction—for instance, away from hysterical overreaction and toward calm modulation. One method is to actively create "thought substitutes" that you use as replacements for your negative or inappropriate self-talk. For instance, if you know that you always react to the arrival of a rejection letter with "This is such a f*&#ed-up business, and I can't take one more rejection!" you can plan beforehand what you want to say to yourself ("Oh, a rejection letter—how amusing!"), and then, when you spot the telltale envelope in your mailbox, *make yourself* think the thought substitute rather than the conventional thought you are accustomed to thinking.

Tactic: Create Thought Substitutes

You can create thought substitutes to replace your negative or inappropriate self-talk. These thought substitutes also serve as simple affirmations and point you in the direction of hope and optimism. With a thought substitute or two at the ready, you instantly replace a thought like "I just made such a big mistake!" with "Let's see if this is really a problem" or "This doesn't faze me a bit" or "I'm just fine." Your particular thought substitutes can be ironic, spiritual, straightforward, or come in any tone or style that suits you. Try creating a few generic thought substitutes that will serve you effectively in toxic situations.

Task: Learning Thought Stopping

When criticism gets under our skin, it can be very hard to silence. A refrain keeps repeating itself: "You are such an idiot, you are such an idiot, you are such an idiot" or "That was so unfair, that was so unfair, that was so unfair" or "You have no chance, you have no chance, you have no chance." At times like this, it is imperative that we silence that obsessive negative thought. We can silence it only by confronting it and shouting "I do not want you, thought!" You can't battle an obsessive thought with a mild-mannered retort. You have to muster your energy, raise yourself up to your full height, and really say "No!" to the thought.

Tactic: Really Say "No!" to a Thought

Think an innocuous negative thought like "What a gloomy day" or "I ate too much ice cream at dinner." Think the thought and then shout, "No!" *out loud*. If the thought wants to return—as such thoughts typically do—the instant you hear it shout, "No!"

again. Feel unembarrassed and adamant. Do not let that thought return without rebuking it and fighting it tooth and nail.

Task: Learning Not to Dwell on Criticism

It is a bad habit of an anxious mind to dwell on negative thoughts. Someone criticizes us and we dwell on that criticism for days and weeks, even though we know that we ought to move on. Or we turn a piece of mild criticism into dramatic self-criticism and beat ourselves up nonstop, day and night, until finally we manage to bring on a good-size depression. A vital cognitive skill to learn is how not to dwell on thoughts that we know ought to be put to rest. But doesn't trying not to dwell on a thought cause you to think that thought? Indeed it does. That is why you will want to employ powerful thought substitutes to help you let go of the unwanted thoughts that plague you.

Tactic: Say, "What's Next?" or "Move On!"

When you notice you've been dwelling on a piece of criticism or self-criticism, internally shout, "Move on!" Or matter-of-factly demand of your mind, "What's next?" Or try saying "I have better things to think about!" or "I'm done now!" or "Time to switch gears!" Whatever thought substitute you choose to use, make sure you have one handy and actually begin to employ it when you find yourself dwelling on criticism.

The Personality Key: Tasks and Tactics

There are scores of ways of conceptualizing personality, from ancient systems, like the medieval one that posits four basic personality types (the four humors), to contemporary systems, such as the Jungian model based on dualities such as introversion and extroversion. There are Freudian drive theories having to do with the interaction of psychic parts (id, ego, and superego), narrative theories that argue that we are the stories we tell about ourselves, personality trait theories based on the idea that we are collec- tions of traits, and many more.

In excess of a hundred personality traits have been identified and described, the seminal concept of ego means something different to each theorist, and influential factors like culture and genetics must somehow be factored into any comprehensive theory of personality. It would therefore not be surprising if you felt you had no very sure way or very clear way to think about your personality—and therefore little idea how to change it or improve it.

Nevertheless, we are obliged to figure ourselves out. You can't deal effectively with toxic criticism if you aren't aware of how you typically act and react in life and if you have no decent sense of what motivates you or what subverts you. As difficult and elusive as personality may be, you nevertheless have certain tasks you need to master if you are going to stand in better relationship to criticism.

Task: Appraise Your Own Personality

In my experience there are certain keys to personality—among them the extent to which a person experiences anxiety and how that anxiety is manifested, has an existential or conventional view of life, is plagued by or free of depression, and so on. Your job is to decide for yourself what the keys to personality are in your case. Have you been made by your culture into a certain kind of person? Did the messages you received in childhood shape you? Were you born with a certain primary personality such that at your core you are pessimistic or optimistic, weak willed or stubborn? Who are you? You really need to know.

Tactic: Write Your Autobiography

In working with therapy clients and creativity coaching clients for more than twenty years, I have found that perhaps the most useful tactic for self-exploration is to write an autobiography of twelve to fifteen pages. If you do, you are almost certain to learn a great deal about who you are. Focus on going deep and being real, not on beautiful memoir writing. You do not need to arrive at a one-word or a one-sentence answer to the question "Who am I?" Where you want to arrive is at a sense of what motivates you, what subverts you, and why you react in the idiosyncratic ways that you do.

Task: Appraise What Criticism Triggers in Your Personality

Some people get angry when criticized and lash out at someone other than the person who criticized them. This psychological defense—where you attack a safe target like your child, rather the person who criticized you, like your father or your boss—is called *displacement*. Other people, troubled by doubts about their abilities, get ashamed and mortified and shrink away. Some people move quickly to depression; others feel goaded by the criticism to act ruthlessly; others treat the criticism as gospel and keep trying to reshape themselves according to what others tell them they ought to do. How do you react to criticism?

Tactic: Complete the Sentence "When I'm Criticized, I _____."

A straightforward way to determine how you react to criticism is to try your hand at completing the sentence "When I'm criticized, I _____."

You can refine your self-examination by completing the following sentences:

- "When I'm surprised by criticism, I _____."
- "When I have the chance to prepare for criticism, I _____."
- "When I'm criticized by someone I thought was on my side, like a friend or loved one, I _____."
- "When I'm criticized by a stranger or someone I consider an enemy, I _____."
- "When I'm criticized about something where I've invested meaning, like my writing if I'm a writer, I _____."
- "When I'm criticized in an area that holds no meaning for me, I _____."
- "When I'm criticized at home, I _____."
- "When I'm criticized at work, I _____."
- "My most usual response to criticism is _____."
- "My most troubling response to criticism is _____."

Task: Learning to Change Personality

If you are brave enough and wise enough to appraise your personality, determine what motivates you and subverts you, and arrive at some conclusions about what personality changes you want to make, you still are confronted by the enormous challenge of actually changing your personality. Say, for example, that you recognize that you grow meek and compliant whenever you are criticized, can trace that reaction to childhood dynamics, and know that you want to change your reaction pattern and the underlying personality piece that produces that reaction. How can you translate that excellent understanding into action? Three steps are required. You must:

1. State a clear goal with nameable behaviors.
2. Practice those behaviors.
3. Act as you have practiced when a real situation arises.

Tactic: Name, Practice, Act

First name a personality goal, such as that you intend to become more assertive. Next articulate what behaviors go with that goal (that the second Jim criticizes you, you will tell him to stop; that when Mary makes a comment about your weight, you will let her know that she is never to make that remark again; that when Barry complains that his socks come out of the dryer full of static, you will turn the laundry chores over to him with great glee). Next rehearse in your mind's eye what you will say to Jim, Mary, and Barry when they criticize you next. Last actually respond as you intend to respond the next time you are criticized by one of them.

Task: Consolidate Personality Change

It is splendid to act assertively when we have decided that we want to become more assertive. But if our habit is to be meek, our style is to be meek, and a host of personality pieces collude to make us meek, then a single assertive response will not do the trick. We need to repeat our desired behaviors over and over, forgive ourselves when we slip and react too meekly, continue practicing and rehearsing, and pay attention to our goals every single day. Just as sobriety is a process and not an event, so too with any personality change that we hope to make. We stay focused on our intentions, cherish our successes, and remain mindful of the fact that slips remain a persistent possibility.

Tactic: Ceremonially Honor the Process

Since personality change is a process and not an event, it is hard to honor it with markers like annual anniversaries. You could certainly celebrate the one-year anniversary of the day you asserted yourself or the day you shrugged away some noxious criticism, but it makes more sense to regularly honor your efforts without connecting your ceremony to any particular event. For instance, once a month celebrate in a small, meaningful way the fact that you remained mindful about being assertive. During your celebration, name the personality change that you are honoring: "Another disciplined month!" or "Another sober month!"

The Behavioral Key: Tasks and Tactics

Much of what we've discussed has to do with "in the mind" matters: formulating your meaning-making goals, honing your appraisal skills, consciously constructing a certain attitude, getting a grip on your cognitions, and so on. The sixth key, by contrast, has to do with your behaviors and your actions in the world, with the concrete ways you present yourself, the concrete things you say, and the concrete actions you take.

Task: Behave and Respond in the Moment

Someone criticizes you. Because you have been working on the cognitive key and the personality key, you are able to control your self-talk and your personality and respond exactly as you intend. What is your best response? In many cases, it will be to say nothing and shrug off the criticism as irrelevant and unimportant. In some cases, however, you will want and need to respond actively. Then your best response is likely to be a brief, clear, affirmative response, affirmative in the sense that it affirms your right to exist and your right to be treated fairly. At the same time, you will want your response to be modulated enough that you don't burn your bridges.

If your mother calls you fat, your response might be to reply calmly, "Never call me fat again." If your editor pans your current fiction manuscript, your response might be to reply calmly, "Let me think about what you said and get back to you tomorrow." If your coworker says, "Because you've missed so many days lately, I've gotten really jammed up," your response might be to reply calmly, "I'm really sorry about that." In each case you offer a brief, clear, measured response that is neither an assault nor a self-attack.

Tactic: Practice ABC Responses

Imagine a negative remark or two that is likely to come your way, maybe from a boss, coworker, or one of your parents, and create and practice some affirmative, brief, clear responses that you might actually use. Get a clear picture of how you want to feel, what facial expression you intend to wear, what tone of voice you want to employ. Try out several responses for each imagined situation, as your first attempts may fall short in terms of brevity, clarity, or power. For each situation, write out the response you like the best and practice it and memorize it.

Task: Ventilate Pent-Up Emotions

Even the most calm, phlegmatic individual still experiences the buildup of stress and needs a repertoire of stress management tools to deal with the rigors of modern life, even if those tools are as simple and straightforward as hot showers and walks by the beach. Similarly, even someone who has evolved a persona relatively impervious to criticism experiences a cumulative buildup of toxins from criticism received.

It is important to learn to ventilate these pent-up emotions in safe, modulated ways. You can ventilate your pent-up emotions by silently screaming (that is, by screaming without uttering a sound, a technique actors use to reduce anticipatory anxiety while waiting in the wings), by pounding a pillow or hitting a punching bag, through traditional talk therapy or via therapeutic massage, by having a good cry, or, of course, by using the tactic discussed in Chapter 2, writing ventilating "Dear critic" letters.

Tactic: Write "Dear Critic" Letters

While you read about "Dear critic" letters in Chapter 2, you may not have tried your hand at writing one yet. Right now, try writing a "Dear critic" letter addressed to someone from the past whose criticism still hurts or to someone you anticipate will criticize you in the future—like your new boss or an art critic. Although gaining insight is the primary goal of writing "Dear critic" letters, an important secondary goal is to vent and to let the toxins escape from your system. Do not underestimate the importance of this venting. Be sure to cultivate the habit of getting things off your chest by regularly writing "Dear critic" letters.

Task: Identify the Actions You Need to Take

Your boss tells you that unless you increase your productivity you will not be offered a new contract or given a raise. This is criticism that is hard to ignore, unless you are intending to leave your job. Because you have trained yourself to deal effectively with criticism, you do not overreact, beat yourself up, let the shadow side of your personality take over, or in any way sabotage yourself. Instead, you calmly appraise the situation. What is going on? Is your boss actually saying something about you, or is he paving the way for handing your job over to his nephew? What is your best understanding of the situation?

Having done your best to understand the situation, which process may include bravely chatting with your boss and getting amplification and clarification, you then identify what actions you need to take to reach your desired outcome (which may be retaining your current job or finding a new job). You effectively deal with this criticism not by sticking your head in the mud or by swallowing the criticism but by identifying the actions you intend to take that will render the criticism moot—and by then taking action.

Tactic: Do the Work Directly in Front of You

It is brave of us to identify the actions we need to take and even braver to actually take them. One technique for taking necessary action is to say, "I am ready to do the work directly in front of me." Announcing our readiness in this way helps motivate us and gets us up and out of our chair. It also helps prevent us from making excuses. The strength and simplicity of announcing that we have work to do that is "directly in front of us" makes this an ideal technique to use when we want to consolidate personality change and get things done.

Someone criticizes you. From our discussion, you have a sense of what you need to do to minimize the impact of that criticism. You need to be so firmly on your path in life that most criticism amounts to little more than the buzzing of gnats. You need to appraise a given situation at top speed and decide whether, and to what extent, you want to bother with this particular piece of criticism. You need to have a philosophical, phlegmatic attitude in place that serves as your own personal nonstick coating. You need to manage your thoughts and your self-talk so as to make sure you don't turn molehills into mountains. You need to manage your personality in such a way that you retain control of your responses, heal from past injuries, and grow in meaningful ways. And you need to act effectively, both in the moment and after the fact. Beyond all this, which is plenty, you need one more thing, without which all the rest hasn't a leg to stand on: you need to get out of the habit of criticizing yourself. That is the subject of our next discussion.

To consider

- What are your meaning-making goals in life?
- What prevents you from accurately appraising situations?
- What in your current attitude makes you most vulnerable to the sting of toxic criticism?
- Do you have the sense that you understand what motivates you and what subverts you?
- Have you ever stopped to listen to what you say to yourself? If you haven't, are you willing to listen now?
- What is the difference between reacting and taking action? In difficult situations, do you typically react or take action?

To do

- If you feel equal to it, try out all the tactics in this chapter at least once. Or pick one task and tactic from each key to focus on, practice it, and begin to incorporate it into your way of being.
- Identify the issue in this chapter that you know is going to give you the most trouble and create a plan for dealing with that issue.
- Create several thought substitutes or affirmations that you can employ to prevent criticism from becoming self-criticism.
- Identify one change you would like to make in your life that will make you less vulnerable to criticism, write out your plan for making that change, and follow your plan.

4

Silencing Self-Criticism

What is the relationship between the criticism you receive and the kind you inflict on yourself? Why do so many people inflict daily doses of criticism on themselves in neurotic ways —that are patently unjustified, unhealthy, and self-sabotaging? To what extent does a penchant for self-criticism turn uneventful episodes of minor remarks into toxic, wounding events? These are the tangled matters we examine next.

Criticism arises because human beings have opinions, make judgments, carry grudges, and act cruelly. For example, you may get yelled at simply because an angry shopkeeper needs some-one to lash out at and today it is you. Criticism arises because of supply and demand and competition and for reasons having to do with survival and scarce resources. For example, you may get criticized because a magazine can accept only one of the sev-eral hundred stories it receives and so rejects you in the natural course of doing business—which rejection you internalize. Crit-icism arises because human beings set up social systems and adopt roles, such as the policeman who admonishes you for going seventy miles an hour when you are supposed to be going sixty-five—even though he himself goes seventy all the time. The structure of human personality, human organizations, and Dar-winian dynamics of competition and survival cause censure to pour in.

Swimming in a Sea of Criticism

Advertisers subtly criticize us for the smells in our house (which their product will eradicate), for the yellowness of our teeth (which their product will eliminate), for toying with the lives of our children by not buying their "safe" tires or their "safe" car. For a full twenty years (if we do some graduate work in addition to elementary school, middle school, high school, and college) teachers are there to critique us through harsh grading or by pointing out our lack of knowledge and ideas. Parents often do little else but criticize their children—noticing them only when they are making noise, not eating their peas, wasting hard-earned money, or not doing their homework. This is the human psychosphere, the psychological bubble that surrounds our every move and is saturated with criticism.

Many of the reasons for this rampant, ubiquitous criticism are sinister. Millions of workers in sweatshops worldwide are criticized for "going too slow" or for "taking too many breaks" so that they will feel coerced to do the work of three people. To exert their power and maintain control, clerics mercilessly criticize their billions of parishioners as sinners or potential sinners—admonishing them for everything from eating unblessed pizza to facing in the wrong direction while praying. To maintain their authority, conscienceless politicians disparage their citizens for rightly disapproving of them. An enormous amount of the criticism that human beings receive is calculated censure arising from the self-serving needs of tyrants who operate openly in every sphere of life.

There are two basic reactions (with a million variations) to this avalanche of criticism. One child who is repeatedly told, "You are too loud!" will internally respond with "F**k you!" A second child will respond with "I must be too loud." The first child runs around like a madman, being as loud as he can be, and the second child becomes meek and quiet. The first child grows a lax conscience—if he grows a conscience at all—and becomes the next sweatshop magnate, ruthless politician, arrogant clergyman, or mass murderer. The second child grows a punitive conscience, becomes a self-critic, and, in the natural course of events, is meekly bullied and controlled by the first child, who is now his pastor, boss, or president.

In this oversimplified model, one person becomes relatively conscienceless and another person becomes a fierce self-critic. By virtue of the interaction between the criticism received during the formative years and the person's particular personality, each individual will incline more toward either sociopathic behavior or self-flagellation. Those who have become even mild self-critics will continue to berate themselves in the absence of any new criticism from the world and take the information received from others as new opportunities to criticize themselves.

The Moment of Translation: From External to Internal Criticism

You send a portion of the novel you have written out to a hundred editors, all of whom turn around and reject it. Eighty-five of them say nothing in particular as they reject it, and fifteen excoriate it. You could feel criticized, or you could say, "They have no idea what they're talking about." Either could be true, and history has proven that the second is a real possibility.

Even though fifteen editors have passed judgment on you as they rejected you, that criticism is nothing like the truth, nothing important, until you take their comments *into your being* and feel criticized. Until that "moment of translation," from external message to internal reaction, their responses were more like news than barbs. Only when there is an internal movement—from their judging your novel to your judging your novel—does the experience of criticism begin to exist. That doesn't mean their comments are not important, that being rejected doesn't disappoint you, or that your philosophical, phlegmatic persona may not take a hit by virtue of all of this rejection. It also doesn't mean there aren't many actions you might want to take, from rewriting your novel to submitting it to European editors with a different sensibility. What is vital to say, however, is that you and you alone get to decide whether you will criticize yourself on account of what others have said to you.

Take a second example. Like a huge percentage of Americans, you may be overweight. For the sake of our discussion, let's pick a number: you are forty pounds overweight. You may or may not be causing yourself health problems at your current weight, though that is a real possibility. You may or may not be negatively affecting your romantic relationships, though that is another real possibility. What is almost certainly true is that you are not happy about the way you look. Like many people, your bottom-line feelings with respect to these forty pounds are likely to be that you are an undisciplined, slothful, hopeless, unlovable pig. And like many people, you have translated those forty pounds into full-blown self-criticism. What you want to say to me with all your heart is *I deserve that criticism!* It seems to you that not condemning yourself would be the height of dishonesty and that, even if you are obese, at least you are forthright.

You opt for self-criticism in part out of heroism, because you believe you have only two choices: to admit what feels like an incontrovertible truth, that you are fat, or to lie about it. But there is a third path that is the key to eliminating self-criticism. It is being truthful but not critical. You acknowledge that you are forty pounds overweight and that when you grow anxious, restless, or bored you turn to pretzels, which you know is a problem. That is, you acknowledge everything—*without at the same time criticizing yourself.* You tell the truth, but you do not slap yourself around.

You may have trouble taking this point in. Since it is among the most important points in the book, I want to repeat myself. You can keep a thought ("A hundred editors rejected my novel," "I am adopted," "I am forty pounds overweight") that customarily turns itself into toxic self-criticism ("I am a terrible writer," "I am so unlovable that even my birth mother didn't want me," "I am an undisciplined pig") from becoming self-flagellation if you decide against allowing it that privilege. You can go from the thought "I am forty pounds overweight" to toxic self-criticism— or not. It is absolutely your choice.

Self-Criticism as Honorable Reality Testing

When we do something that we aren't proud of—that we know we shouldn't do—and admit that fact to ourselves, that admission feels honorable (if also painful). It feels honorable to notice forthrightly that we haven't written in a month or that we've recently gained ten pounds. We know that if we denied this truth and took the route that so many people take of refusing to notice or acknowledge their shortcomings, we might avoid self-criticism. But we prefer honesty. Accordingly, we take toxic self-criticism as almost a tonic, as the medicine we are obliged to swallow for failing ourselves. The matter seems simple and straightforward: "I bravely admit that I avoided my writing for no good reason, and now I must feel guilty, embarrassed, even humiliated. That is the adult thing to do. I have no choice but to call myself a weakling and a failure, predict ongoing malfeasance, and arrive at the bottom-line conclusion that I am essentially no good. If I am being real, what choice do I have but to arrive at such conclusions?"

Our apparently righteous decision to criticize ourselves for our shortcomings seems all the more righteous by virtue of the fact that the people whom we disrespect—serial killers, pedophiles, abusers, sociopaths, narcissists, tyrants, and everyday defended people who lie to themselves and others—do not criticize themselves, do not take responsibility for their actions, do not feel guilt or remorse. If it is the hallmark of people we definitely do not want to be to refuse to pass judgment on themselves, then it seems to follow that remembering to criticize ourselves is our moral duty. It seems as if we manage to further distinguish ourselves from the people we disrespect by vehemently calling out our shortcomings.

Without quite realizing that we are thinking this way, we view self-criticism as a badge of honor and our moral responsibility. If we haven't lived up to our standards, we had better let ourselves know it and, as righteous and appropriate punishment, rub that news in. It doesn't feel like quite enough moral approbation just to point out that we could have played the piano beautifully if we had continued practicing: no, we have to conclude that observation with "You hopeless idiot!" It doesn't feel like enough to admit that we haven't found our path in life and that we haven't tried that hard to look. We have to end that disclosure with "You pathetic weakling!" We habitually move from unfortunate fact to self-inflicted wound. We think we are being honorable and engaging in appropriate reality testing when we notice our shortcomings and then censure ourselves for them. Even if we are practicing Buddhists and can quote chapter and verse on detachment, even if we are practicing cognitive therapists and can quote books on maladaptive thinking—even if we know better, it is hard for us to arrive at this hard-won truth: self-criticism is not righteous; it is only a mental mistake.

Self-criticism is a mental mistake rooted in the way that the mind readily turns mere problematic information—such as that you are speaking at a certain high-decibel level—into self-chastisement: that you are speaking too loudly. Because you are built to make this mental mistake, you regularly commit what philosophers call the naturalistic fallacy: you turn an "is" into an "ought." "I am speaking at XX decibel level" is an "is," a natural fact. "I am speaking too loudly" is a statement about right and wrong, about what is proper and what is improper. To move habitually from a fact to a negative self-judgment without noticing that you have cavalierly attacked yourself is the epitome of neurotic self-harm.

Self-Criticism as Mental Mistake

The truth will set you free. But smacking yourself in the mouth as you tell yourself the truth will only break your teeth. There is no good reason to move from an accurate appraisal of a given situation, even if that accurate appraisal casts you in a negative light, to self-criticism. Did you do something cruel? Don't criticize yourself; instead make amends and refrain from further cruelty. Did you ruin a meal? Don't criticize yourself; instead forgive yourself and move on. Did you make a wrong choice and end up in a career you loathe? Don't criticize yourself; instead change careers. Criticizing yourself adds nothing high-minded or useful to the situation.

Consider the difference between the first and the second reaction to personal shortcoming in each of the following pairs of reactions:

> **A:** "I haven't written in a month, and I'm an idiot."
> **B:** "I haven't written in a month, and I will start writing right now."

> **A:** "I am forty pounds overweight and a hopeless slob."
> **B:** "I am forty pounds overweight and about to do something about it."

> **A:** "I messed up the best opportunity for advancement I will ever have, now I'm trapped in a stupid job, and I couldn't have made a bigger botch of the whole thing if I had actively tried to ruin myself."

B: "I messed up an excellent opportunity for advancement, I am grieving the fact that I wasn't able to rise to the occasion, and now I will have to make the best of the situation."

Let's look more closely at this last example. You were given an opportunity for advancement, and for some reason you blew it. Maybe it was bad luck; maybe it was self-sabotage; maybe you weren't ready to take the next step. Whatever the reason, the fact remains that you are back in your old job and now feel trapped, disappointed, despairing, and full of self-loathing. You hate where you are and can barely tolerate coming to work; and you hate yourself and can barely tolerate looking in the mirror.

Which is more disturbing to you, the reality of the situation and the fact that you are trapped in a job that you hate, or the way you failed yourself and what that says about you? If it were the latter, that would be one thing. But what if it is the former, which is actually quite likely? What if what most disturbs you is still coming to work at this job that you hated before and that you now hate even more? If in fact this *is* what is disturbing you, then adding on self-criticism is surely a mental mistake. You are better off figuring out how to leave or better the situation.

Is self-bashing somehow a useful motivator? Your argument that it is might go as follows: "The more guilt I can generate and the more I can make myself feel like a fool and a failure, the more likely I am to turn myself around. If I merely note that I made a mistake, I could easily ignore that observation, but if I add on that I am a pathetic, helpless cretin, I am bound to feel more motivated to do whatever it is that I now need to do." Does this make sense? I don't think it does. I don't think anyone genuinely believes self-criticism is an effective motivator. To be sure, it sometimes seems that we need to "hit bottom" before we can stand up, which suggests that until we deeply acknowledge our shortcomings and surrender to the fact that we haven't been living wisely, we can't move forward. But in fact hitting bottom isn't a moment of heightened self-criticism. It is a moment of profound self-acceptance and optimism. It is a moment when you awaken to the knowledge that you must stop all your squirming, struggling, denying, and self-criticizing and step onto the path of taking new action.

There look to be no conceivable circumstances where self-criticism is a truly useful add-on. It seems to be much more a personality-driven bad habit and mental mistake. Yet, because it is such a ubiquitous phenomenon, it pays to ask the question one more time: since there seem to be only negatives associated with passing judgment on yourself, and since people nonetheless keep routinely and roundly criticizing themselves, might there be some hidden "positive" reason for remaining attached to these self-attacks? Is there some subtle something that we gain or achieve through self-sabotage? It turns out that often there is: self-criticism can serve as a nice dodge, as a handy way of avoiding the hard work that comes with trying to live an authentic life.

Self-Criticism as a Dodge

Self-criticism can serve as one of the ways that you avoid doing much harder things, like making an effort and inaugurating change. It can arise out of weakness and serve your shadowy need to let yourself off the hook. It is strange but true that you may find it easier to condemn yourself for not writing than to sit down and write, easier to call yourself fat rather than diet and exercise, easier to say you are a failure rather than try to succeed. Self-criticism can prove a comfort and serve as a handy excuse.

Our inner talk often seems to proceed along the following lines: "I haven't written very much, and the little I've written has been on balance pretty bad. I think maybe I could write quite well, but I could be wrong, and I don't think I really want to find out because I might end up with something that I probably couldn't sell or humiliate myself by writing drivel. Sure, I could try to maybe do the remarkable thing of writing something excellent and seeing it published, but that seems so unlikely that I think I would rather skip trying. Since I can't just skip trying, as that would feel too cowardly and disappointing, I need to actively excoriate myself for not writing. If I do this enough, it should drain me of any residual desire or lingering energy that might be available for writing and, by putting me in such a dark place, guarantee that I won't write. Sounds good. Let me violently castigate myself and then get on with what I really want to do, which is anything but write."

Embedded in this common way of thinking are many of the ideas we have discussed already with respect to the six keys. Our self-critical writer has not actively chosen his path or committed to his meaning-making goals. He has not adequately appraised the situation or adopted a useful attitude in life. He is clearly not aware of how his self-talk operates and has not wrested control of his thoughts. Nor is he in charge of his personality or willing to take the kind of action that would amount to useful change. In addition, he is a textbook masochist: he deals with his rampant anxiety by inflicting pain on himself. Given his lack of self-awareness, his self-sabotaging patterns, and his penchant for masochism, it is no wonder that he "gets so much" out of criticizing himself.

Being Truthful but Not Critical

As long as you hold it as sensible to criticize yourself for making this or that big mistake or for failing yourself in this or that big way, you will continue to do so. The alternative to self-criticism isn't denial or a merry relinquishment of power and control. You don't say, "I never make mistakes," or "Yes, I haven't done the things I wanted to do, but that must be what the universe wanted of me." The first is denial, the second slavishness. You say, "I haven't done the things I wanted to do," and you end that with a full period. You name the truth, feel the pain if there is still pain, but refrain from criticizing yourself. Then you continue with "And?"

You name the truth and then ask yourself what you want to do. What if the truth is just too awful: that by failing to carefully watch your child, she was run over and killed; that by acting out for one split second with a choreographer, you ruined your chances for a dance career; that all the writing you have done for the past fifteen years has been irredeemably bad; that your miserable personality has cost you a lifetime of love? Even if the truth is this horrible, self-criticism adds on nothing of value. "I acted out and ruined my chances" is bad enough. How are you helped by adding "And let me beat myself up about that until the end of time"?

The truth is bad enough. The truth about the situation in Africa, whether you want to look at poverty, malaria, AIDS, famine, drought, warfare, or something else, is bad enough. "And I am a bad person for not doing anything about that situation" does not add on anything of value. Saying "And?" and meaning it does. The "And?" means "What do I want to do about this hard truth?" Your answer might be "I want to do this." Your answer might be "I don't know precisely, but I will think about it." What it can't and shouldn't mean is "And I will continue to beat myself up about it—and about the failing ozone layer too."

It is important that we separate the pain we feel because something happened from the activity of criticizing ourselves. If your child was run over and killed because for too long a moment you chatted with your neighbor and failed to notice your daughter drifting out of the front yard and toward the street, you will have to endure the pain of her absence forever. But that is entirely separate from having to blame yourself forever. The pain is unlikely to go away. The self-criticism must. If every time you experience this pain, you mentally move to guilt and self-chastisement, you are making a mental mistake of the most horrifying kind.

Our job is to keep a thought, any thought ("How horrible a time Africa is having!" or "I am fully forty pounds overweight") from turning automatically to self-criticism, and also to keep a feeling, any feeling (pain, anger, envy, resentment, disappointment) from triggering self-criticism. We are so used to moving from a certain kind of thought and a certain kind of feeling directly to self-criticism that separating them at the hip may feel impossible. But until you can do that, you will live a half-incapacitated life.

Self-Criticism and the Six Keys

No matter how accusatory the thought or how dreadful the feeling, you do not allow that thought or that feeling to glide into self-criticism. You can see why committing to eliminating self-criticism necessarily returns you to the six keys. You refrain from criticizing yourself because:

1. Self-criticism does not help you achieve your meaning-making goals or aid you in leading an authentic life.
2. Self-criticism does nothing to help you appraise situations.
3. Self-criticism is in conflict with the philosophical, phlegmatic attitude you have decided to adopt.
4. Self-criticism is maladaptive self-talk that only serves to weaken and incapacitate you.
5. Self-criticism is a shadowy part of your personality and one of the ways you avoid facing up to life's challenges.
6. Self-criticism is not a motivator but a disincentive to act.

It is hard, verging on impossible, to effectively handle censure if you regularly turn information from the world into self-criticism. Insofar as you are prone to excoriate yourself, you will also be prone to interpret innocent or neutral comments as criticism, magnify the importance of mild criticism, and in a variety of ways pile it on your own head. Honesty and self-criticism are two different things: an honest appraisal of a flaw leads to useful action, self-forgiveness, or some other beneficial outcome; criticizing yourself for the flaw leads to inaction and depression. There is nothing noble or righteous about self-criticism. Let it go.

To consider

- Despite my analysis, you may still feel that self-criticism serves some useful purposes. What are those useful purposes, and are they really the fruit of self-criticism or the fruit of something else, like honesty or bravery?
- Even if you agree that self-criticism serves no useful purpose, you may believe that eradicating self-criticism is beyond the power of anyone but the most advanced master. Do you believe that eradicating self-criticism is within your power or beyond you?
- If you suspect that silencing self-criticism is in fact within your power, what will it take for you to accomplish that remarkable feat?

To do

- Explain in your own words to what extent self-criticism does or doesn't serve a useful purpose.
- Create a simple but robust plan for silencing self-criticism.
- See if you can think a self-incriminating thought without going directly to self-criticism.
- See if you can feel a painful feeling (like disappointment) without going directly to self-criticism.

5

Putting Criticism in Context

Criticism does not exist in a vacuum. I experience everything according to my needs, my personality, and my construction of meaning. For example, my experience of you criticizing the war our country is waging is likely to change after my son is killed in that war or after damaging government documents are exposed. My experience of you criticizing me for my weight is likely to change after I have shed a hundred pounds and have come within ten pounds of my target weight.

From the subjective perspective of a given person, every situation is unique. Therefore, at the heart of the appraisal process is the understanding that there is no good way to respond in a rote manner to the criticism we receive. The same sort of rude rejection letter will have one meaning if it is the first such rejection letter you have received or if it is the thirtieth. If it is the first, you might be inclined to say, "This has no meaning. I will just send my story out again." If it is the thirtieth, you might be inclined to say, "Sending out my story this way appears not to be working. I need to do something new, either by rewriting it or by changing my marketing efforts." There is nothing different about the two letters; the situations are different.

The primary thing that makes one situation different from another is "where your head is at" when you receive that critical comment or remark. Consider a typical, everyday situation. You prepare a recipe for the first time. It turns out poorly. Your spouse criticizes the dish—and, by implication, you. A month later you prepare the dish again. This time you understand the process better and the food is delicious. Again your spouse criticizes the meal—and, by implication, you. Same spouse, same criticism, different situation. Last month you might have wondered, Am I really a bad cook? This month you have to wonder, Do I really have such a cruel spouse?

Given the virtually infinite number of elements that might define a given situation—your current construction of meaning, your mood, the exact wording of the criticism, the tone in which the criticism is delivered, even the look of the sky—how can you possibly effectively appraise a situation so as to know what is really going on? The answer is, by virtue of your brain, the most sophisticated collection of matter in the universe. If you are willing to apprehend the gestalt of a situation, if you have the courage to look situations squarely in the eye, and if you are committed to making sense of your reality, you have a brain that will do the work.

Let's examine some situations carefully, so as to get a clear idea of how you can appraise what is going on even though you are enmeshed in the situation. What we are trying to answer is the following question: how can we apprehend the reality of a situation even as we are living it? It turns out that we can train ourselves to appraise situations, even as we live them, if we follow a few specific rules.

"Your Tone Is Very Thin": Criticism from a Teacher

Consider the following situation. You are a twenty-year-old conservatory student studying the oboe. Among the pressing matters on your mind are that you suffer from performance anxiety, you doubt that you play well enough to become a principal player, you aren't happy with your expensive but not top-of-the-line oboe, and you have some serious doubts about whether you really want to devote your life to music, even though you love music and music making. You could have been a doctor (that is a self-critical thread, that you passed on medicine), you could still become a lawyer (that is a second self-critical thread, what you call your "indecisiveness"), and now you have a big audition coming up for the main conservatory orchestra.

As preparation for that audition, you have some extra lessons with your oboe teacher. He is always critical, but he is more critical these days, probably because the audition is approaching and he recognizes that more is at stake. You come in for your 4:00 P.M. lesson and play. After a while he stops you abruptly and caustically says, "Jane, your tone is very thin!" He has said this to you before, but today it feels like a stab to the heart. Silently you disassemble your oboe, clean it, put it away, and leave a full twenty minutes early. Your only thought is "I hate it here, and I want to leave."

Recognize the Real Issue

You have been criticized, and you experience the criticism as toxic. But your experience of the criticism as toxic has little to do with the comment itself. It has to do with the totality or gestalt of the situation. You have arrived at a moment when the criticism inflames conflicts that have been simmering within you for a long time, makes a particularly pressure-filled audition feel ever more difficult and dangerous, and in a cumulative way calls into question the path you are taking in life. Therefore, it is a heart rocker.

Every situation is a complex puzzle. Two of the puzzle pieces at play for you in this situation are the following. First, do you actually want to become a professional musician? Second, is your tone so thin that you can't succeed as a symphony performer? The first is part of your simmering existential conflict; the second is a reality-testing issue in the world of music. If you answer no to the first question, the second question becomes moot. If you answer yes to the first question, then the answer to the second question rises to the level of vital significance. Nor is it easy to see which you should try to answer first, as your ability to honestly answer the second may be impaired by the simmering existential conflict and your ability to honestly answer the first may be impaired by your doubts as to whether you play well enough to succeed.

Rather than try to answer either question first, you must do exactly what I just did: spell the issues out. That is what the mind is made for, to spell issues out. You say to yourself, "If my playing is so poor that I can't make it as a classical musician, then that's decided. But what if I could improve my playing, or what if it isn't actually that bad at all? If I had an objective answer about that or could accurately predict what my playing would become, then at least I would know if a musical career is a possibility. Let's say that I could answer that question. Let me travel down each road in my mind, depending on the answer. If I learn that my playing is not good enough and will never be good enough, what do I want to do then? And if I learn that my playing is good enough or could become good enough, what do I want to do then?"

Consider It a Blessing in Disguise

This is how you appraise a situation. The criticism is the spark that ignites the examination. In that sense it is a blessing, as it may spare you two decades of auditioning for but never getting hired by a great symphony or point you in the direction of the things you need to do to succeed as a musician. Criticism never feels like a blessing, but, because it can provoke exactly the examination that you needed to undertake, it may serve as a needed catalyst for self-examination and change.

You were not a blank slate when your oboe teacher said to you, "Your tone is very thin!" You were someone in conflict about your life purposes, confused about whether you loved music enough to devote your life to it, uncertain about whether you had it in you to play well enough to become a symphony musician one day, and much more. Into this roiling complexity came some acidic words: "Your tone is very thin!" Naturally they had the potential to cause an outsize reaction in you, as you were already in crisis.

Use It to Reexamine Your Life

If you do not take this as an opportunity to make sense of your situation, you are likely to take these words as criticism of the most toxic sort, get depressed, beat yourself up, and maybe even make a precipitous decision to leave the conservatory. If you do take this as an opportunity to better understand your current situation and resolve the conflicts roiling inside of you, you can take your teacher's words, which surely were meant as criticism, as the opportune spark that ignites in you the desire to understand what is true for you.

You screw up your courage and use your brain. What outcomes are possible from this difficult, righteous work? You may have to finally confess to yourself that you don't play the oboe well enough to achieve your grandest dreams, that you never will play that well, and that you can only end up in a second-tier orchestra. You may suddenly realize that this outcome is perfectly fine, that playing the oboe in any orchestra and getting paid to play is better work than any other work you can imagine. Or you may decide that it is time to choose a new path in life. In the moment, this analysis will feel scary and horrible, but at the end of it— whatever you decide—you may experience real closure and relief.

Honoring and analyzing the complexity of a situation is the epitome of living authentically. You can see why it often feels easier to take the criticism and get depressed than to do this authentic work. Accepting the criticism and the resultant depression at least doesn't embroil you in having to decide whether or not to make enormous changes or entail that you really look at your strengths and weaknesses. Those activities might lead to honest grief, so we are likely to opt for everyday depression instead. By forgoing that real examination, we fail to resolve our conflicts or give ourselves the chance to live at peace.

If you stop to make sense of your teacher's criticism in the full context of your life, rather than reacting to it with pain and sorrow, you have a chance at good news as well as bad. Yes, you may learn that you must bite the bullet and decide about your life as a musician. But you may also learn that you love music so deeply and trust your ability as a musician enough that you are willing to risk continuing. If you arrive at this conclusion, then, heart in hand, you might return to your teacher and ask, "How can I achieve a fuller tone? Because I want to make it as an oboist!" Who knows—your teacher might even reply, "Oh, I didn't mean that it was *really* too thin. I was just motivating you!"

"You Are So Boring": Criticism from Your Spouse

Consider a second example. Joanna is a stay-at-home mom raising two young children. She is college educated, worked in the world as a project manager, and was successful and accomplished at her work. Now she devotes herself to her home life. Part of her is happy with this arrangement, feels fulfilled by it, and finds meaning in it, and part of her is bored silly by the endless routine of dishes, laundry, cleaning up, and baby talk. Every day tires her out, but in an unfulfilling way.

To counteract the inanity of her days, she participates in play groups, has other mothers over for coffee, and in a variety of ways tries to fill her day with more than diapers. These efforts, though, are usually less than successful. When her husband comes home from work, which often isn't until seven or eight in the evening, she really needs him to be present and available, as he brings with him stories from the world and a whiff of freedom.

Roy, however, usually comes home tired and out of sorts. He interacts with people all day long, has to wear a false smile and mouth company policy for eight hours straight, and when he gets home wants only a drink, food, and television. Aggressive and ambitious, he is nevertheless bored with his life, his wife, and his children and has been chatting up a woman at work, preparing for an affair. Because this affair is brewing, he has trouble looking his wife in the eye or even being in the same room with her. So he usually makes straight for the den when he gets home, both to get some peace and to keep from having to interact with Joanna.

Don't Avoid the Real Issue

Joanna and Roy bicker and, without being able to put her finger on the source of his mood, Joanna is aware that Roy is unhappy, absent, and unwilling to talk to her about anything. She fears that his unwillingness has a lot to do with the fact that she has nothing interesting to say and no ideas in her head. She tries to be bubbly as she reports about the children and her day with them, but she recognizes that her reports aren't interesting even to her. When those reports fall on deaf ears, she tries to extract some news of his day and the wider world from him, but his invariable response is "That's the last thing I want to talk about!"

Joanna feels Roy's criticism of her, but his criticism is rarely voiced. One evening that changes in a dramatic way. He comes home from work, takes his dinner into the den, and after a bit she visits him, hoping for a chat. Instead of wearing his usual aggravated, absent look, he looks colder and more focused than usual. She knows that something is up but has no idea what it might be. Nervous, she begins to tell her husband about her day, about what Melanie said and Randy ate. Suddenly Roy shakes his head and says, "You are *so* boring."

Take a "Ten-Second Pause"

Joanna flees the room and in the privacy of the bedroom bursts into tears. Because she feels bored and boring, Roy's criticism rings true. If she is unlucky enough not to think contextually about Roy's toxic comment, she may bad-mouth herself into a depression or an eating binge, rush out to buy some books to read so that she can become (or seem) more interesting, complain to a confidant who, never having liked Roy, immediately suggests a divorce, or stuff the comment only to find herself in bed with the flu two days later.

In addition to working the six keys, Joanna needs to step back and put Roy's comment in context. Joanna will find this extremely hard to do, as her body is flooded with feelings and her mind is racing. But it is the very best way for her to proceed. First, she needs to calm herself. This she can do by taking some deep breaths or, better yet, by using the breathing-and-thinking technique called the *ten-second pause*, where she uses a deep breath ten seconds long as a container for a calming thought like "I am perfectly OK" or "I trust my resources." Once she has calmed herself, she can begin her contextual analysis.

Find Meaning in Your Life

This contextual analysis would sound something like the following: "Many things have been going on between Roy and me and inside each of us individually. I don't really know what's on his mind, and, as angry as I am with him, I had better find out. More important, I had better find out what is in my own mind. His charge that I am boring exactly dovetails with my own feelings about my life. One issue is him, another issue is the two of us, but the first issue is me. I love the children, and I don't hate my life. But I am bored, undernourished, underutilized, and not very happy. The first step in whatever it is that I plan to do has to be figuring out how I can construct a less boring life and still do justice to my responsibilities. Where does that train of thought lead me?"

Joanna sleeps on her question "How can I construct a less boring life and still do justice to my responsibilities?" and in the morning awakes to the understanding that the work she previously did in the world lends itself to a consulting business that she can run from home. Instantly, she worries that she would be taking on too much by starting such a business, that she would further resent Roy if she had to maintain all her current chores and a new business as well, and that starting such a business, no matter how careful she might be, would shortchange her children. She sits with these objections throughout the day, holding them seriously but lightly, and by the middle of the afternoon has made up her mind.

Her first step, she realizes, is to stop feeling bored herself. If not feeling bored makes her less boring, excellent; but the primary reason for starting a home consulting business is to provide herself with a more meaningful life, one that makes use of her skills, talents, and intellect. She therefore decides that she will start the consulting business. She knows that her second step is to make sense of her relationship with Roy, a step that she will need to get to quickly, as his cutting criticism is proof that their problems are escalating. First things first, though; scared but excited, she begins to plan her consulting business.

"Please Stop Writing": Criticism on Your Art

A third example will complete our brief examination of the contextual nature of criticism. Jack has been writing for two years and has just completed his first novel. Like most first novels (and like most novels in general), it has some strengths and quite a few weaknesses. Like all novels, it will appeal to some readers but not to other readers. Jack, of course, isn't able to take this sort of objective stance with respect to his novel and holds a hope and a fear: the hope that his novel is great and will be snapped up and the fear that it is lousy and will be roundly criticized.

Jack screws up his courage and begins to approach literary agents with a query e-mail. Many don't reply, and, of those who do, most don't ask to see his work. Of the twenty-five agents he queries, three ask to see a novel synopsis and a portion of the novel. Jack sends these materials out. So quickly that it seems that she couldn't possibly have read it, one agent returns his package with a form rejection. A week later a second package is returned, again with nothing but a form rejection letter included.

Don't Turn to Despair

Down to the last of these twenty-five agents, Jack is already irritable and despairing when the last package slides through his mail slot one afternoon. In it are his query letter, novel synopsis, sample chapters, and another form rejection letter. Scribbled at the bottom of the rejection letter are a few words from the literary agent: "Please stop writing!" Jack can hardly believe his eyes. He has to read the words several times to digest their horrible message. When they finally register, it is like a dagger to the heart.

If Jack has not cured himself of letting toxic criticism affect him, any one of several terrible outcomes are likely. He may rush to agree with the agent that he is a no-talent fool who ought to stop writing, put the novel away in the back of the closet, and never write fiction again. He may try to deny what he just read and find himself "blocked" for the next decade, neither revising his first novel nor getting beyond twenty or thirty pages on his next novel attempts. He may let loose some shadowy part of his personality, the part that is ready to attach to an addiction, and start drinking or gambling heavily. If he is not prepared for this existential blow, this meaning crisis may derail him.

Giving Yourself an Honest Assessment

If he is prepared, if he has worked the six keys and knows to engage in a contextual analysis, he will also know to say something like the following to himself: "This is the first novel I've written. Two things are probably true about it, that it is not good yet and that, with rewriting, it either can be good or can't be made good. Even if it can't be made good, all that means is that I've spent a year as an apprentice and now get to start on a second novel. That is not a tragedy, and to make it into a tragedy is to mismanage my self-talk. What I must monitor is that part of me that wants to agree with this agent and throw in the towel. That is the gravest danger I face right now, that I will use this agent's criticism as ammunition to shoot myself down. I know that part of me is always ready to give up, and this is a perfect opportunity to do just that. I can't let that happen!"

Take Action to Make Constructive Changes

Having had this brilliant chat with himself, there are any number of "behavioral key" actions that Jack can take. He can bravely reread his novel and make it better. He can make copies of the novel and enlist three friends to read it, inviting their feedback— that is, their criticism. He can try twenty-five more agents. He can revise this novel and also start a new novel. Unless he intends to make meaning elsewhere, what he must not do is take this criticism to heart and fear that he has no future.

A criticism feels significantly more painful if it both criticizes us in the moment and also drives a stake through our future. It is one thing to have our novel rejected. It is another thing to read in that criticism the fact that we will never have anything published. As you tackle the contextual analysis of the criticism you receive, remember to ask yourself, "Am I extrapolating from this criticism that I am doomed?" Criticism that feels the worst is criticism that looks as if it will be true for all time.

What is absolutely certain is that a criticism of the sort that Jack received, which denies him a future, is completely invalid. No piece of writing that we produce, however horrible, proves that we have no chance at a writing career. No editorial comment on a particular piece of writing, however scathing, can be treated as gospel. If Jack allows this editorial comment to rob him of his future, that must be considered his choice and his decision. In context, it means that he was ready to resign.

Going Back to the Six Keys

You put criticism in context by returning to the six keys. First you ask yourself, "Does this criticism connect to the way I intend to make meaning in my life?" If it doesn't, you slough it off. You are done with it. You are sufficiently in control of your attitude, your self-talk, your personality, and your behaviors that you just snap your fingers and let the criticism evaporate.

If a piece of criticism does not connect to the way you intend to make meaning in life, allow it no meaning. Consider it irrelevant and make it irrelevant. If you take in criticism that you know has no real meaning for you, if it is only a little hurtful and a little upsetting but otherwise irrelevant and you continue to hold it to your bosom, you aren't in sufficient control of yourself. The problem isn't the criticism but rather your reaction to it.

If the criticism does connect to the way you intend to make meaning in life, as it did for Jane, Joanna, and Jack, then courageous appraisal is the key. You must step back and put the criticism in context. This means examining the situation with honesty and insight. You may learn hard truths and set the stage for changes that you don't really relish making. You have no choice, however, as criticism this important is going to provoke some large reaction in you one way or the other.

Rather than reacting defensively and impulsively, rather than stuffing the criticism and getting weak and sick, rather than lashing out or opting for denial, you acknowledge that you have no choice but to honorably appraise the situation and put the criticism in context. Your existential health depends on it, as this piece of criticism has attacked you on the level of meaning. You look "Your tone is very thin," "You are so boring," or "Please stop writing" squarely in the eye and bravely commit to a thorough contextual analysis.

To consider

- When you are criticized in such a way that you have no choice but to address the criticism, what mechanism or language will you use to remind yourself to engage in a full contextual analysis of the situation?
- Do you have the patience and fortitude to engage in the kind of contextual analysis we've been discussing? If not, can you map out a program for change that would allow you to grow into someone who can step back and take a wide-angle view of situations?

To do

- Think of a time when you were criticized. Engage in a retrospective contextual analysis. See if you can put that criticism in context, taking as broad a view as possible.
- The next time you find yourself criticized, say to yourself, "I am going to put this criticism in context." Notice whether some of the sting of the criticism doesn't instantly evaporate when you make that announcement. Then get out a pen and a pad and bravely analyze the situation.

6

Fair Versus Unfair Criticism: How to Tell the Difference

There are many tricky aspects to the appraisal process. It is often very hard to know what our life purpose and our life path are and therefore hard to know whether a given criticism is existentially relevant. Likewise it can be difficult to fathom the content of our thoughts and the quality of our feelings and therefore hard to judge the exact nature of the thoughts and feelings that a given criticism provoked. But no aspects of the appraisal process are trickier than the following pair: getting a handle on what we mean by "fair" and "unfair" criticism and, more important, getting beyond whether a given criticism is fair or unfair and plotting a course of action based instead on what serves our interests.

What do we actually mean when we say that we were "fairly criticized" or "unfairly criticized"? Unfortunately, we tend to mean a variety of very different things. When we say a criticism is unfair, we typically mean one or more of the following: that our critic got his facts wrong; that he is offering up mere opinion as fact; that he has an agenda; or that the remark was delivered in a cruel, rude, or otherwise "unfair" way. Thus we might dub each of the following unfair: to call our hair short when it is objectively medium-length, to say that we invariably look better with our hair long when we know that the way we look is a function of much more than our hair length, to bring the matter up at all, and to deliver the message snidely.

What about the following? What if an editor tells us there is no audience for a novel that is as long as ours, in essence criticizing our effort. Is this a fair criticism? Well, if this is her true belief and it is also an accurate appraisal of the marketplace, perhaps, though it is hard to suppose that a blanket statement of this sort could ever be 100 percent true. So, is it fair? It's hard to say. But what if she is using our novel's length as an excuse to turn us down because she is tired of trying to launch the careers of first-time novelists? If the phrase is in a code that we do not understand, how unfair is that? We hoped to get a plain-English response like "I am very tired of trying to get first-time novelists launched, so I am passing," and instead we get "Your novel is too long for the marketplace." The criticism is unfair—and we don't even know it!

Separating Fact from Opinion

This should hint at the complexities we face as we try to gauge whether a given criticism is "fair" or "unfair." What, for instance, is a factually accurate or inaccurate criticism, given that so much of it is mere opinion? How does intention factor in: is a criticism less fair if it is factually accurate but delivered just to insult us? What if one part of a criticism is accurate but another part—the more important part—is inaccurate? What about word choice and delivery: if inaccurate criticism is delivered gently, does that render it innocuous? If useful criticism is delivered harshly, does that make it unfair?

Consider the ten criticisms in the following sections. When we consider just the "facts of the matter" in each of the following quite simple cases, they may seem overwhelming. When we try to factor in the speaker's intention, which we may not be able to gauge, and delivery style, which may so upset us that we can't think clearly, we should feel less than sanguine that we can ever judge the absolute fairness or unfairness of a given criticism.

1. School Administrator to Classroom Teacher

"You teach your classes in a rote, mechanical way that doesn't allow for student interaction, and that isn't the way we want our teachers to teach."

Which facts and opinions are up for grabs? These three, to begin with:

- I teach my classes in a rote, mechanical way.
- My teaching methods do or don't allow for student interaction.
- The school administration does or does not want all teachers to teach in a certain way.

What intentions might be at play? Any of these three, among many others:

- This administrator doesn't like me and is looking for a way to criticize me.
- This administrator has been told by an accrediting committee to "encourage student interaction" and so is doing just that, without his heart being in it.
- This administrator has been told that he must cut ten teachers and he is looking for "cause" to release me.

How might this criticism be delivered? In any of the following ways, among many others:

- Calmly, neutrally, and on balance sympathetically
- Curtly, loudly, and in front of passing students
- In harsh language of the "you always" and "you never" sort

2. Writing Teacher to Writing Student

"The way your story opens, with a tough guy being nice to a mutt, is such a cliché that nobody is going to be able to take the rest of the story seriously."

Which facts and opinions are up for grabs? These three, to begin with:

- A tough guy being nice to a mutt is a cliché.
- A cliché is a bad thing in every instance.
- Cliché or not, this is a thing that will prevent readers from taking my story seriously.

What intentions might be at play? Any of these three, among many others:

- This teacher's pedagogical style is to find "one serious error" in every story she critiques.
- This teacher is attracted to me and attacks everyone she finds attractive.
- This teacher views me as an accomplished writer and doesn't want one flaw to ruin my story's otherwise excellent chances.

How might this criticism be delivered? In any of the following ways, among many others:

- In an encouraging way, of the "Your story is excellent but one thing about it troubles me" sort
- In a blistering way, of the "You can't write for beans and here is one proof of your lack of talent" sort
- In a neutral monotone

3. Wife to Husband

"I wish you wouldn't take Bobby hunting today—it's such a barbaric sport."

Which facts and opinions are up for grabs? These three, to begin with:

- I am taking Bobby hunting today.
- I am taking Bobby along so as to teach him to hunt, as opposed to taking him along for, say, company.
- Hunting is a barbaric sport.

What intentions might be at play? Any of these three, among many others:

- My wife is jealous of the time I spend with my hunting buddies.
- My wife, a vegetarian, is adamantly opposed to hunting.
- My wife fears that I might do our son Bobby, whom I didn't want, "accidental" harm in the woods.

How might this criticism be delivered? In any of the following ways, among many others:

- Angrily
- Plaintively
- Fearfully

4. One Politician to Another

"Atheists like you aren't real Americans!"

Which facts and opinions are up for grabs? These three, to begin with:

- I am an atheist.
- Someone gets to decide who is a real American.
- This politician gets to decide who is a real American.

What intentions might be at play? Any of these three, among many others:

- He wants to deflect us from a debate about issues.
- He wants to appeal to his religious base.
- He wants to appeal to my religious base.

How might this criticism be delivered? In any of the following ways, among many others:

- Trumpeted, with flags and drums
- Quietly, with actual conviction
- Sarcastically, in a long string of accusations

5. Younger Sister to Older Sister

"Nobody in the family has ever cared about me, and you've been the worst! What kind of sister are you?"

Which facts and opinions are up for grabs? These three, to begin with:

- No one in the family has cared about our sister.
- I have been the worst in this regard.
- A sister ought to be a certain kind of person who holds her siblings in high regard, whether or not they deserve that high regard.

What intentions might be at play? Any of these three, among many others:

- She wants to make me feel guilty so that I will offer her a place to live.
- She is desperate and about to harm herself.
- She is playing a tape that has hardly any real or current meaning for her.

How might this criticism be delivered? In any of the following ways, among many others:

- With disappointment
- With dripping venom
- In obvious pain

6. One Friend to Another

"At your weight, you're an embarrassment to your children."

Which facts and opinions are up for grabs? These three, to begin with:

- There is a correct weight for me.
- I weigh more than this absolutely correct weight by some margin that is clearly "too much."
- My children are in fact embarrassed by my weight.

What intentions might be at play? Any of these three, among many others:

- She wants to punish me for sleeping with her husband.
- She wants to relay information that my children have confided in her.
- She wants to motivate me to lose weight.

How might this criticism be delivered? In any of the following ways, among many others:

- Offhandedly
- Pointedly
- Compassionately

7. Floor Manager to Employee

"Everybody else gets seven skirts done in an hour. Why are you doing only five?"

Which facts and opinions are up for grabs? These three, to begin with:

- Everyone else gets seven skirts done in an hour.
- Everyone who gets seven skirts done in an hour is doing a good job on those skirts.
- I get only five skirts done in an hour.

What intentions might be at play? Any of these three, among many others:

- This is a prelude to demanding eight skirts an hour from everyone.
- He is attracted to me and will "forgive me" for producing only five skirts an hour if I sleep with him.
- He is routinely and randomly yelling the same thing at everyone.

How might this criticism be delivered? In any of the following ways, among many others:

- Threateningly
- Loud enough for everyone to hear
- With or without curse words

8. Painting Instructor to Student

"Nothing you've shown me in this class makes me think that you have any aptitude for painting."

Which facts and opinions are up for grabs? These three, to begin with:

- Work done in this class (or in any class) is evidence of whether or not a person has an aptitude for painting.
- This instructor can judge whether or not a person has an aptitude for painting.
- I have worked in a way that would allow this instructor (or anyone) to judge whether I have an aptitude for painting.

What intentions might be at play? Any of these three, among many others:

- I have passion, power, and talent, and he is envious.
- He is dying of cancer and full of bile and regrets.
- He says this routinely to 98 percent of his students because he is a self-styled "gatekeeper of the profession."

How might this criticism be delivered? In any of the following ways, among many others:

- In a group critique session
- Privately, but loud enough for students at the surrounding easels to hear
- In a caustic, biting, sarcastic way

9. *Aunt to Niece*

"You look much better with your hair long."

Which facts and opinions are up for grabs? These three, to begin with:

- I always look better with my hair long.
- I never look better with my hair long.
- I sometimes look better with my hair long and sometimes better with my hair short, depending on many factors, including the goodness of the haircut, my makeup, my weight, what I'm wearing, etc.

What intentions might be at play? Any of these three, among many others:

- I am getting married, and she is a bitter old maid.
- She just read an article about "short haircuts as a sure sign of lesbianism."

- She would genuinely like me to look my best, which in her old-fashioned worldview is with long hair.

How might this criticism be delivered? In any of the following ways, among many others:

- Confidentially
- Bossily
- Publicly

10. Father to Daughter

"Can't you be nice to Miriam? You know that your stepmother only wants what's best for you."

Which facts and opinions are up for grabs? These three, to begin with:

- I am not nice to Miriam.
- This is actually my father's opinion (as opposed to Miriam's opinion).
- Miriam "only wants the best for me."

What intentions might be at play? Any of these three, among many others:

- This is a prelude to sending me away.
- My father has his own doubts about whether Miriam wants what's best for me and is offering me an opportunity to talk about it.
- My father is trying to placate Miriam so as to give himself time to extricate himself from an affair.

How might the criticism be delivered? In any of the following ways, among many others:

- Plaintively
- Imploringly
- Angrily

Given that every criticism is a problem in logical analysis and a psychological mini-drama, is it really possible to come to a clear conclusion about whether a given criticism is fair or unfair? Our temptation is not to bother and to sidestep the matter entirely. Your aunt says something about your hair: you ignore her comment and cross her off your Christmas list. Your boss tells you to make seven shirts an hour instead of five: you endeavor to raise your rate without wasting time on analysis. This is the usual way.

Putting Criticism Behind You

Unfortunately, sidestepping the issues that a given criticism raises isn't good policy, whether you err in the direction of ignoring the criticism or in the direction of taking the criticism to heart. John, a writer, provides an excellent example of one sort of danger associated with a lack of analysis. John explained:

> My wife, June, also writes fiction. In the first workshop she'd ever been a part of, the teacher, an award-winning short story writer with a lot of success in the academic fiction writing world, questioned one element of June's story that they were "workshopping." There was a rubber chicken in the story, and for some reason this bothered the teacher. He told June and the class that no one would publish a story with a rubber chicken in it and asked June if it couldn't just as easily be a doll.
>
> This completely destroyed June's confidence in the story and her desire to work on it. The rubber chicken was central to her conception of the story. To her, it absolutely could not be anything else. But at that point in her career she didn't have the confidence to reject such a criticism from someone with so much apparent critical authority. She put the story away and still hasn't revisited it, though she vows she will now that she has more confidence in her ability and sees how unfair the criticism was.

Having thought about it for a while, I do think that my wife found it very hard to take the advice objectively. That is, she might have been able to get something useful out of the criticism—she might have thought about the comment "objectively" and tried to get something that could really help her with the story. She might have thought, "OK, the chicken is throwing him. How could I sell the chicken; how can I make it work?" but she couldn't because the comment struck so much at the heart of her inspiration for the story.

It felt, I think, like a trespass or an attempt by the teacher to dismiss her. As I say, the man was competitive, and it's easy for me to see how she'd feel attacked and put down rather than offered real help. But part of it definitely was how she took it. This suggests the question "How can you not take this sort of thing so much to heart?"

Staying Focused on the Six Keys

The first step in dealing with criticism of this sort is *letting go entirely of the notion of fairness and unfairness.* You are not trying to judge something as simple as whether the ball a batter hit is fair or foul. A criticism delivered your way is not "fair" or "foul"; it is a statement uttered by one human being toward another human being in a complex contextual field. The criticism may be factually accurate but interpersonally foul, objectively inaccurate but revelatory, and so on.

Forget entirely about "fair" and "unfair." Is a factually inaccurate criticism leveled at us by someone who loves us and who wants to provoke us into useful action "unfair"? Is a factually accurate criticism that we can do nothing about and that is delivered our way just to insult us "fair"? These aren't the questions to ask. Our only good strategy is the one that I have been advocating all along, one that is far more difficult than "embracing fair criticism" or "ignoring unfair criticism." It is working the six keys and putting each criticism in context.

Criticism Provokes New Understanding

Jeremiah is a well-known southern painter who paints in the realist tradition and specializes in nature painting featuring animals in the wild. He has been painting this way for thirty years, commands top prices for his canvases, teaches classes worldwide, and writes a monthly newsletter on art-related matters that goes out electronically to several thousand subscribers.

In one issue of his newsletter Jeremiah recounts a recent experience. A gallery owner had asked him if he had any "very small paintings" available, and this got Jeremiah to thinking about a technique that he had used twenty years before and had never returned to, that of cutting a small square out of a mat and using that square to "look for" interesting abstract bits "hidden" in larger paintings that, for one reason or another, hadn't turned out well.

Jeremiah experiments with this technique, cuts out a number of abstract squares from a pair of large canvases, frames the abstract squares, and presents them to the gallery owner, who loves them, shows them, and sells them. Jeremiah himself is pleased with them, though in a wry way, as cutting squares out of unwanted canvases doesn't feel like the epitome of art making and, more poignantly, because he senses how these abstractions are at least as powerful as, if not more powerful than, his best, most fully realized realistic paintings. He manages to put these thoughts aside and gets on with his realistic painting.

Several months later Jeremiah encounters an article about him in an art magazine. Titled "Abstraction Trumps Realism," the article recounts Jeremiah's experiment with abstract squares. The author concludes that not only is Jeremiah the abstract artist stronger and more interesting than Jeremiah the representational artist but that, as these results prove, abstraction is the greater art. The author manages to get many of his facts wrong and is so curtly dismissive of Jeremiah's realistic work and realism in general that it feels easy to write this off as a "sloppy hatchet job." But Jeremiah isn't inclined to dismiss the author as unfair. Nor is he inclined to agree with the author's conclusions. What he feels is provoked.

Jeremiah feels provoked to understand for himself why those small abstract paintings felt so powerful and whether their undeniable power should cause him to disavow realism and turn to abstraction. For several days he mulls the matter over in a state that can only be described as agitated. The question is important to him; the answer may cause him to turn in a new direction and even repudiate his life's work. Then, on the fourth morning, he has a revelation.

Abstraction may be powerful, even supremely powerful. But provoking a powerful response in the viewer is not all that he is after. He wants a child of the city to know the settling of birds and the slithering of snakes. He wants to show real things, in real settings, as he experiences them. He has always wanted this; nothing about his foray into "cut abstraction" has changed his basic intentions, aspirations, or preoccupations. Jeremiah can smile and now really put the article behind him.

Letting Go of "Fair" and "Unfair"

When you are criticized, you want to know how to react. How you react shouldn't be a function of whether the criticism is fair or unfair, accurate or inaccurate, kind or cruel. Rather, your reaction should be a measured judgment of the criticism in context. This measured judging includes discerning the accuracy of any facts put forward (is every seamstress in the shop producing seven skirts an hour?); separating putative fact from mere opinion (is it really a fact that an interactive style is the appropriate way to teach differential calculus?); weighing subtexts, agendas, and anything else that contributes to the context; and then making a decision based on your best interests, not on your seething emotions.

We needn't bother ourselves about whether a criticism is fair or unfair. If editors tell you that your novel has no shot at an audience but their dismissal is just code for "I'm not interested," is that fair? It doesn't matter! What matters is that you figure out the truth of the matter. What matters is that you come to a conclusion about whether your novel has a shot—and, if it does, what you need to do to get it that shot. If your sister is correct in her appraisal that you haven't been on her side, should you feel guilty because her appraisal is "accurate" or "fair"? No! What matters is whether she deserved your support and deserves it now. Words like *fair* and *unfair* and *accurate* and *inaccurate* only make it more difficult to judge situations contextually.

When you are criticized, your task isn't to figure out if the criticism is fair or unfair. Your task is to figure out *what the criticism means in context* and *what you intend to do* based on your contextual analysis. Jeremiah could have called the article that panned his subject matter and his style "unfair," since it contained enough inaccuracies and biases to float a battleship. Or he could have found himself agreeing with its main contention, that the abstract squares were more visually arresting than the painting they came from, dubbed that criticism "fair," and arrived at a place of doubt and despondency. Either dismissing or embracing the article's contentions would have amounted to an incomplete and unfortunate result. What Jeremiah needed to do, and what he did do, was not stop when he encountered something "unfair" or "fair" in the criticism but continue to think the matter through all the way to the end.

To consider

- When you can't tell for certain if a criticism is accurate or inaccurate, what will you do?
- When you can't determine the intentions behind a criticism, what will you do?
- How will you separate the delivery of a criticism from its content?
- Do you agree that a criticism's "fairness" or "unfairness" is a secondary matter and something of a red herring? Put this idea in your own words so that it sinks in at a deep level.

To do

- Bring to mind a criticism from the past, one that you consider particularly unfair. Think through how you might have handled that criticism if you had focused not on its unfairness but on what was in your best interests to do.

Part 2

Deflecting Criticism in All Areas of Your Life

7

Criticism from Family and Loved Ones

Wounds left by critical remarks from parents, siblings, a spouse, or children are sometimes the hardest ones to heal. The criticism leveled by parents—beginning in infancy and continuing throughout our years at home—strikes when our personalities are forming, when we are most vulnerable. It has the greatest potential for harm of all the criticism we receive. Sibling criticism also cuts deep. Our siblings sleep in the next room, even in the next bed, and know too much about us. They know the mistakes we make, the things we fear, the dreams we hold, and vie for the same love and resources. When they disparage us, they come at us both motivated and well armed.

Criticism from a mate is toxic in special ways. This is a person who, unlike members of your family of origin, you have invited into your life. With your mate you have double-barreled criticism to bear: your mate's and your own for being the sort of person to allow criticism into your own bed. Nor is anyone privy to more ammunition. Given the magnitude of our shortcomings and the number of our secrets, a mate who wants to pass judgment can acquire enough ammunition in a day to last a year.

The criticism that our children level at us has its own great potential to cause harm. Our children can make us feel guilty simply by criticizing themselves. When your child says, "I'm a failure," you say, "I failed." A child who says, "I'm a failure and it's all because of you!" is only saying something you are already thinking.

All in all, the people closest to us, if they choose to be critical and cruel, can be the most dangerous people in our life.

Peeling Away the Layers: What Are They Really Saying?

Nowhere is the contextual nature of criticism clearer than when it comes from those we love. Behind every not-so-innocent remark—from a mate's "Where did you hide the peanut butter?" to a mother's "Aren't you going out tonight?"—is a world of history, injunctions, and complications. These can paralyze us as our anger butts up against a slew of half-conscious thoughts—that it's their right to criticize us, that the remark might be for our own good, that the drama would escalate if we confronted them, or that we might lose our loved one if we stood our ground.

If responding directly and forcefully to the underlying message behind "Where did you hide the peanut butter?" might cost us our marriage, it is no wonder that we are inclined to reply, "Right behind the jelly, dear." We decide that discretion is the better part of valor, find a way to deny that we were just belittled and criticized, and continue our safety maneuvers. We say something sweet and mild when our mate continues with "Have you paid the bills yet? You always let them sit around so long!" We know we want our peanut butter–hunting mate to do three things: First, to find the peanut butter. Second, if that's not possible, to say, "Love, do you have any idea where the peanut butter might be?" rather than accusing us of hiding it. Third, and most important, to change altogether into someone who is not accusing us, abusing us, or holding us in low esteem. Because this third outcome is what we really want and because we doubt that we can get there by responding to the remark in an assertive way, we let our mate's veiled criticism pass by unrebutted. The result? Virulent toxins circulating through our system nonstop.

There is very little that's simple about the criticism we receive from family members and loved ones or about our reactions to those comments. Powerful, shadowy, vengeful, and envious feelings may be at play, as well as deep-seated issues of authority and control. Despite all these difficulties and complexities, the appropriate path is obvious: you work the six keys. By working the six keys you become someone who not only responds appropriately and effectively to the criticism but is savvy enough, strong enough, and brave enough to deal with the underlying dynamics.

What do these complexities sound like in real life? Here are three brief reports. The first is from a young woman reflecting on her beautiful stepsister's comment "Oh, your hair looks fine." The second is from an abused daughter scolded and criticized by her narcissistic mother for refusing to attend a family reunion. The third is a "Dear critic" letter written by a blocked writer to his deceased father.

"Oh, Your Hair Looks Fine"

The comment comes unsolicited as my stepsister and I both stand before mirrors in the ladies' room of a restaurant before joining an annual family gathering. It's a damp, windy evening and my brown hair needs a brief reordering, even if I do wear it short. I'm just running my fingers through to enliven it when my stepsister makes her remark. Immediately I know she means, among other things, "Your hair is hopeless, and nothing you can do is going to make you look good." Her own naturally blond hair falls to her shoulders in thick waves, and she tosses her head as if there were a man around to seduce. (She always stays in practice.) And as clearly as if she had said it aloud, I seem to hear my stepsister say, "Nobody is ever going to pay any attention to you, so why bother?"

Years ago, the first night we had to share the same bedroom—we were both age eight—my stepsister established her superiority. She threw me out of the bed, pushed me out of the room, and locked the door. This was her father's house, and I'd better remember that I was only the daughter of the wicked stepmother. I soon learned that she was her father's darling and a truce was possible only as long as my stepsister occupied the center of the universe.

It's been a long time since we've had to inhabit the same house, and I've gone on to graduate from college and start a career, while my stepsister has had to get a restraining order to keep her ex-husband at bay and beg her father for money to travel back home with her two children. She has no job qualifications and hates the menial work she now must do. But none of this matters. I leave her still primping at the mirror and join the gathering, my arrival barely noticed. As soon as my blond stepsister appears, all heads turn.

"Don't You Always Do What You Want?"

I've just told my mother that I'm not coming to the family reunion this year. We don't discuss the matter during this phone call, but I already know that in her opinion this lapse is a dereliction of duty. What I'm hearing beneath the words she speaks is "You abandon me! After all I've done for you, you don't love me enough to do just this one little thing."

Almost from the moment my own father died (I was age three), all the relatives and neighbors told me, "You must be good to your poor mother." She was a young widow with two children, and it's true that she experienced many mishaps. Even after my mother remarried, people kept telling me how I must always help my "poor" mother, how I must never cause her more difficulty. In my childish mind, the idea grew that another disaster would befall us all if I did not obey my mother.

Meanwhile, my mother framed all her requests as "If you love me . . . ," usually shouted in an angry-sounding voice. "If you love me, you'll get out of bed this minute!" "If you love me, you'll eat the rye bread and milk so your daddy [stepfather] will not get angry." Among other tyrannical rules that my stepfather decreed (no apples allowed in the house, everyone must stir sugar into their stew before eating), the entire family had to consume rye bread and milk every Saturday night. I nearly choked on rye bread and milk, but every week I ate it anyway so as not to cause my mother any trouble—and because she asked me to (after all, I did love my mother then, though a time would come when I would have to wonder). Years later she will still say to me, with what reaches my ears as a tone of accusation, "Don't you always do what you want?"

"You Have Failed in So Many Ways"
Dear Dad,

It's been a year since you died, yet I still find myself thinking of how you criticized me while you were alive. It started when I was very young. "Why do you always have to learn everything the hard way?" you used to ask, as you stretched me across your lap and whipped me with your belt.

The worst of these episodes came one horrible evening—I was in elementary school, nine years old—when I refused to eat the chili Mom had cooked (I didn't like the taste or texture). You criticized me for turning my nose up at "perfectly good food" that you would have been thrilled to eat back during the Depression, when you were my age. You threatened me with your belt until I ate a big bite. After I threw up, you screamed at me and whipped me as I cried. Later, as your drinking went out of control and you went bankrupt, after I had started experimenting with pot, you called me a hypocrite for daring to criticize your alcoholic drinking, which by then had cost you your business and fortune, including the money you and Mom had put away for my college education. You brought this up again, too, last year, when we saw you before you died.

In my early twenties, when I was first trying to get started as a creative writer, after I graduated from college, working part-time here and there instead of taking a career job to make time for writing, you ridiculed me for not having published anything and told me I'd never be a success, that I was stupid and foolish to try, I didn't have any artistic talent, I was ruining my life; and you made it clear that this was just part of the larger disappointment you felt about me. I had been given a great gift of intelligence, and I was wasting it. I was a failure in your eyes.

I hope you can look down and see the way I still suffer inside sometimes, how often I find myself feeling small and helpless and worthless, just the way I did when you used to criticize me and scream at me and beat me with your belt. I hope you can feel how much I needed your love and approval instead of that criticism and punishment. And I wish you could do something to help me in those moments, that somehow you would be able to let me feel love from you instead of that hate and pain. But I know that's just a fantasy. I have to handle this myself somehow.

Here I am, fifty-two years old, still trying to write the novel I've had on my desk for too many years now, one unfinished draft after another. I'm afraid I can't write it. I'm afraid if I do write it, it will be no good. Damned if I do and damned if I don't. And I know that if you are watching me now, you're ashamed that I haven't been able to make more of a financial and material success in my life and that I haven't even been able to follow through and realize those artistic dreams that you knew—yes, you knew and you told me so, often enough—I was foolish to entertain.

I wish I could have learned more from your love and less from your harsh criticism and bad example. I wish you hadn't criticized me so often and unfairly. And I really, really wish I could let go of this and set myself free to create, free of the fear of criticism—fear of your criticism. And I know how pathetic it is to whine this way— it's the ultimate proof that you were right, of course. I can't do anything right, just the way you said it.

Your son,
Rob

Applying the Six Keys to Family and Loved Ones

Let's carefully examine how you can deal with the criticism meted out by those closest to you. First, you should already be working the six keys. You will need to have a good, or at least decent, understanding of how you intend to live your life, some willingness and expertise in contextually appraising situations, a more philosophical, phlegmatic attitude in place, a better grip on your self-talk, a decent understanding of how your personality operates, and the savvy and courage to take necessary action. That is a lot, but it is also what is required of you if you are to cure your vulnerability to toxic criticism.

Applying the Existential Key

Let's take a look at Mary, a forty-five-year-old college-educated homemaker, former dancer, and current would-be writer, married to a software engineer, with two teenage children. Mary lives at some distance from her mother and stepfather, whom she avoids seeing as much as possible because she finds them toxic. Knowing she will next see them at Thanksgiving, which is two months away, she makes the decision to spend the next two months preparing herself in ways outlined in this book.

She intuitively recognizes that this regimen may prove scary and daunting, since there is a built-in demand that she look at herself and at her life choices, but she has the feeling that a self-examination of that sort is exactly what she wants. After all, she doesn't just want to deal better with criticism. She also wants to loosen the grip of a persistent, low-grade depression so she can feel better about herself and her life. In short, she wants a real makeover. She reckons that choosing to deal more effectively with the criticism that will come her way in Boise is a good way to start this makeover.

She begins by sitting with a pair of existential questions: "How do I currently make meaning in my life?" and "How do I want to make meaning in my life?" The questions confound and disturb her, because she begins to realize that she has done something like "abdicate meaning making" in the course of doing all the things that have grown up around her, like being available for her husband, Frank, when he's around the house, ferrying thirteen-year-old Jessica and fifteen-year-old Bill to their various activities, maintaining a toe in the dance world by sitting on the board of the community dance company, visiting with friends several times a week, and taking care of the repetitive chores associated with running a house and feeding a family.

Applying the Appraisal Key

Some of this she begrudges, and some of this she enjoys. None of it, however, quite makes use of her mind, heart, or soul or really engages or enthuses her. She begins to see that she has had this problem all her life, the problem of walking a path without sufficient depth and interest to feel meaningful. Maybe there is no such path; maybe her life is exactly as it ought to be; maybe the real task is to change her attitude and to feel more grateful, more satisfied, and more settled. Agitated, she wrestles with these thoughts for several days.

This examination causes her to look at her chaotic childhood, which included a verbally abusive father whom her mother divorced, a lecherous stepfather, and a mother who just couldn't be trusted. Mary begins to see that each of these three pivotal figures felt free to criticize her and that she grew up in a cauldron of criticism, which made it virtually impossible for her to feel secure and self-confident enough to meet the challenges of meaning making. It strikes her as no surprise that she has been more a dabbler and a seeker than an ardent worker in some discipline —like writing, which was always her dream.

She suspects that sitting down and writing the novel she's always dreamed of writing is probably a significant part of the answer to how she would like to make meaning in her life. But she can't be sure about that, since she's never given novel writing a serious try. She also has the sense that she would love to be occupied with a job that makes use of her brains and her heart. She can't name that job, however; so that path to meaning has no reality yet. Something else also begins to brew in her: that a deeper relationship with her husband and her children would infuse her life with more meaning. Other ideas pop into her head: that she could be more present and less scattered, more attuned to the beauty and wonder around her, more political . . . finally she has to take a break from this meaning analysis. All she can say for certain is that something positive, scary, and real has been activated by putting the meaning question on the table.

Applying the Attitudinal Key

Next Mary decides to consciously change her attitude. She translates my instructions to become more phlegmatic and philosophical into the following mantra: "Relax. Big things are coming." She isn't sure what those "big things" are, but she knows that something is brewing. By holding the idea that these "big things" are coming, she finds herself less concerned about "the small stuff" swirling around her: about Jessica's complaints that her soccer uniform doesn't get clean anymore, which in the past Mary would have turned into self-criticism of her homemaking skills and her lack of concern for her daughter's well-being; about Bill's complaints about his teachers, which in the past would have made her anxious about Bill's future and then translated into self-criticism of her parenting skills; and about Frank's complaints that none of the big chores ever get done, which in the past she would have taken as criticism of her management skills and lack of handiness.

Applying the Cognitive Key

As she endeavors to change her attitude and let these complaints glide by her, Mary is startled to notice what she's been saying to herself all these years. She realizes that she has never monitored her self-talk or noticed the anxious, negative, and self-castigating nature of her inner conversations. For a few days she tries to hear what she's saying to herself. When Frank complains about Bill's grades, she hears herself say, "I've got to get on Bill's back or he'll be in trouble for college." It suddenly strikes her that she has always taken it as her responsibility to scold, lecture, and mollify the children, even when Frank is the one who brings up the problem. For the first time in their married life, she finds herself not inclined to take on the role of school enforcer. She hears herself calmly reply to her husband's concern, "Yes, you should talk to him about that."

"Excuse me?" Frank replies, caustically enough that Mary hears an inner warning: "Uh-oh, Frank's getting angry." It startles her to realize that she has based so many of her responses on—indeed, has organized so much of her life around—"not making Frank angry." It isn't as if she fears him. But simply to avoid scenes and to protect the illusion that their life together is swimming along on calm waters, she has taken on the job of mollifying Frank. It strikes her that she no longer wants to do that.

"I agree with you," Mary continues. "Bill's grades aren't what they need to be, and you should talk to him about it."

"Why me?"

"Why not you?"

"I don't know," Frank replies. "I suppose I could talk to him."

Applying the Personality Key

Pleasantly surprised by this "easy victory," Mary next tries to tackle the matter of her personality. But she has no clue where to begin. She knows all sorts of bits about herself—that she obsesses about her weight, that crossing bridges makes her unaccountably anxious, that she prefers calm to drama, that she loves time to herself—but those bits hardly amount to a coherent picture or some sort of blueprint from which to work. She has the intuition that trying to answer a question like "Who am I?" or "How do I typically respond to criticism?" won't reveal enough. Finally she bites the bullet and attempts the exercise I recommend of writing her autobiography.

After several false starts, she settles into writing her autobiography. As she writes about her childhood, she begins to get a very clear picture of the forces at play on her personality formation: how the fights between her father and her mother made her withdraw (and ultimately withdrawn), how she slowly but surely gravitated toward the role of peacemaker, how the introduction of her stepfather into the picture stripped her of her last sense of safety and contributed to her doubts that she was entitled to her own voice and her own space. After writing a dozen pages and rereading what's she written, she arrives at a headline description of her personality: "play it safe; don't make waves; don't really exist."

Applying the Behavioral Key

This feels like enough insight and information for the time being. Mary knows what she needs to do: not play it safe, make waves, and exist. This gets her thinking about her behaviors. How exactly does she want to behave? Nothing comes clear as she thinks about this question, but she knows that some behavioral change is brewing. She can't say which behaviors she ought to change or what new behaviors she wants to inaugurate, but she knows she won't be able to deal effectively with the criticism coming her way at Thanksgiving unless she behaves differently. She has the sure feeling that she will.

She finds herself nodding. It won't be enough to walk in with a new attitude, put her mother's criticism or her stepfather's criticism in context, or monitor her self-talk. She must behave differently if the experience is actually to feel different. That will be the acid test: that she act and by acting change the dynamic between her and her parents. Her goals are to reduce the toxic effects of their criticism and, beyond that, to get their criticism to stop. She can feel in her gut how goals of this magnitude are going to require real action on her part.

Thanksgiving arrives, and the family flies to Boise. As usual, her stepfather is the one to open the door and greet them. He hugs Bill and Jessica, shakes hands with Frank, and says to Mary, "Can I get a hug from you? Or are you too grown-up for that?" Mary suddenly realizes that this thematic criticism, that she has always been "snobby and standoffish," is rooted in his predatory sexual nature and her attempts to keep him at bay. All those years that she worried that she was too snobby and standoffish were years wasted on a worry manufactured in her by him, by a prurient stepfather who had sex on his mind. She can feel her face flaming.

Everything about the situation demands that she hug her step-father and everything inside of her is repulsed by the idea. What she hears herself saying is "This clown ruined my chances of ever being intimate." She can't hug him, but she doesn't feel equal to making a scene. So she replies, "I've got a cold!" and waltzes by him. This hardly feels like a victory, but she realizes she has taken a first step in altering her relationship to her stepfather—and maybe a first step in reclaiming her ability to be intimate.

Mary greets her mother, who comes up to her just as Mary is taking off her bulky overcoat. Mary's arm gets a little stuck in the sleeve, and it takes her a moment to fumble the coat off. She notices her mother watching her in that false-friendly, critical, vigilant way and knows for an absolute certainty what her mother is about to say. A second later her mother says it.

"You were always so clumsy!" her mother exclaims brightly, as if offering a compliment. "To think that you wanted to be a dancer."

In the past Mary would have answered, "I *was* a dancer," to which her mother would no doubt have simply shrugged. This time Mary calmly replies, "Why did you say that?"

"Why did I say what?" her mother replies, wearing her company smile, looking a little befuddled and absent—her protective coloring, Mary realizes.

"Why did you say, 'You were always so clumsy'?"

"Oh, I have no idea! Don't take me so seriously! Let's go inside and I'll show you what I've been baking."

Mary recognizes that this is another one of her mother's controlling maneuvers, to play dumb, to put your concerns down, and to whisk you somewhere else. This time Mary is ready.

"You know, you were always so cruel," Mary says.

"What did you say, dear?"

"Oh, I have no idea!" Mary replies, knowing full well that her mother heard her. "Don't take me so seriously! Let's go look at your baking."

Mary is certain that she doesn't want to use irony or to fight fire with fire as long-term strategies. As interim strategies devised on the spot, however, they look to be significantly better than getting beaten up and feeling bad. As Thursday and Friday pass, Mary notices that her mother is holding her tongue. One opportunity after another arises that in the past she would have used as occasion to criticize Mary—the amount of food on Mary's plate (whether a lot or a little), her outfit (whether casual or dressy), or her hair (whether short or long).

I've stopped her in her tracks, Mary finds herself thinking. She really can't help smiling. For the first time in as long as she can remember, when Thanksgiving is over and she is back in her own home, she discovers that she is energized and ready to make some meaning, rather than depressed and ready to take to her bed.

Breaking the Cycle and Living More Authentically

Dealing effectively with the criticism inflicted on you by family members and loved ones flows from living more authentically and more mindfully, not from following some set of rules. You cure yourself of your vulnerability to toxic criticism by cleaning up each relationship, including your relationships with the dead. You proceed by healing where healing is wanted, by severing connections where distance is needed, by having frank discussions, by expressing your feelings, by setting limits, by changing when you are the one at fault, by doing exactly what a particular relationship needs.

Criticism in intimate relationships sounds like "Oh, your hair looks fine," "Where did you hide the peanut butter?" "You were always so clumsy," "Don't you always get what you want?" or "You have failed in so many ways." Whether it arrives as an innocent-sounding remark about our hair or the location of the peanut butter, a hurtful but offhanded remark about our clumsiness, or a full-scale accusation about our selfishness or worthlessness, because it is delivered by someone who is supposed to love us, because it comes at us so intimately and so often, and because walking away is so imperfect an option, it has real power to disturb our sense of self and disrupt our meaning-making efforts.

As such, criticism from loved ones regularly reaches the threshold where it must be addressed rather than swept aside as irrelevant. It affects our psyche; it affects our meaning-making efforts; it reflects negatively on our ability to stand up straight and reach our goals. You do not deal with such intimate, insidious criticism by snapping your fingers and magically eradicating it. You deal with it by working the six keys—that is, by living mindfully and authentically in all aspects of your life.

To consider

- Everyone is occasionally criticized by a family member or loved one. Does the criticism you've received (or still receive) at the hands of family members and loved ones cross the threshold from innocent to toxic? If the criticism you receive is relatively minor and innocent, your best bet may be to sweep it aside as irrelevant. If it is toxic, it must be addressed. In your judgment, which is it?

- Are there areas of thematic, fair criticism that require you to look at yourself and make certain changes?

To do

- If a family member or loved one is in the habit of criticizing you in ways you deem toxic, what do you intend to do? If you can, spell out how you will work each of the six keys in your effort to end this toxic dynamic.

8

Criticism from Friends and Peers

We receive criticism from (and criticize) our friends and peers from our earliest days. Toddlers are already pointing out to each other how things should and shouldn't be done. As we are socialized, so we are criticized. Much of the criticism is graduated: we may not be the best at what we do, but we are also likely not the worst, so we become the kid who is picked third (but not first or last) when two softball team captains choose sides, the kid who comes in fourth in the schoolyard race, the kid whose artwork is hung up but not in as prominent a place as the class's star artist.

We learn about pecking orders and cliques from our first social moments. We learn that doing a certain thing—say, praying in public—gets us snickers from our secular friends, while not praying (so as to cozy up to our secular friends) gets us dirty looks from our praying peers. Almost nothing we do as children, from drawing a horse with five legs to wearing a cowboy vest, from wanting to sing in the Christmas pageant to raising our hand in class, goes unpunished. Some of this criticism we hardly notice; some of it becomes the backdrop of our days and causes us to hate school and to suffer headaches and stomachaches. Some of it entirely changes our path in life.

How Toxic Criticism Affects Us During the School Years

Consider the following "Dear critic" letter from Sarah, who had her youthful desire to become a singer crushed in one memorable childhood moment.

Dear Mike and Timmy,

Kids can be cruel, and I know it. You probably were not conscious of it at the time, but when you teased me for holding my mouth like an opera singer when we were six years old and singing in the school concert, you hurt me deeply. My mother loved opera singers, and I wanted to be one, but your teasing had a powerful effect on me.

You might be surprised to hear that I did not sing from that time on (unless, of course, I could bury my meek voice in about two hundred people). I didn't sing in the shower, I didn't sing in the car, I didn't sing happy birthday to my family. I didn't sing from that time, at the age of six, until I was thirty-five. In December 1995, however, I joined a choir, facing my fear. I sounded like I hadn't sung for twenty-nine years.

I sing all the time now. I call people up on their birthday and sing. They often tell me that they save my message on their answering machine for months. I love singing. I wonder if you realized the impact you would have on me when those words came from your mouths. I forgive you, for kids can be cruel, but it is really amazing what harm one child can do to another.

Sarah

We are sensitive to the criticism of our friends and peers throughout our school years, but the toxic effects of criticism grow as we approach and reach puberty. We feel the sting of criticism each time someone we hope will be attracted to us isn't. We feel the sting of criticism as labels begin to creep into our head, that we are the nerdy one, the bookworm, the oddball, just ordinary, too short, too fat, too ugly, too unremarkable.

This dynamic causes us to feel criticized even on days when our peers have not gone out of their way to criticize us. We watch our friends flirting and being drawn to one another as we walk through the halls like ciphers and feel silently criticized. Here is a "Dear critic" letter from Alan, who still vividly recalls a particularly humiliating incident.

Dear girls whose names I can't remember but whose laughter I can still hear:

It was the winter dance during ninth grade. We were supposed to dress up, and I wore a hand-me-down suit in which I must have looked ridiculous. I didn't want to wear it, and I almost didn't go to school that day. Finally I got it into my head that maybe nobody would notice that it was an old man's suit, that maybe everybody would be feeling awkward dressed up for the dance. No such luck!

Most of the girls were pretty kind and didn't laugh. But the three of you laughed your heads off and followed me around, pointing me out to the whole school. You called me "Grandpa" and "Farmer Al" and some other things I can't repeat. I guess this was all part of the growing-up process for middle-school kids, but I think it set me back so badly that I couldn't make sense of the social scene in high school. Maybe that's just an excuse—all I know for sure is that you made me feel terrible, and while you were laughing I had the sense that something in me was being crippled.

Alan

Why Our Friends Become Our Natural Critics

Developmental psychologists argue that the chief task of our high school and college years is identity formation: we actively try out behaviors and attempt to answer those two poignant questions, "Who am I?" and "What do I want to do with my life?" As we try out behaviors, we gauge how our friends and peers react to them and begin to choose friends and peers so that our behaviors elicit noncritical reactions. If we are drinking a lot, we hang out with drinkers, not because we love their company but because they won't criticize our drinking. If our path requires that we be studious, we choose studious friends; if our path requires that we step outside of conventional society, we identify and associate with outsiders.

As much as we would like to minimize and control the amount of criticism we receive by virtue of how we choose our friends and acquaintances, we remain at risk. Our friends have their opinions, and we have ours. Our friends have their pockets of cruelty, and we have ours. Our friends can be jealous and envious of us, and we can be jealous and envious of them. Their habits can strike us as ridiculous and wrongheaded, as can ours to them. Since familiarity does breed contempt and since close friends feel they have permission to say whatever they are thinking, it is sometimes between the closest of friends that the most toxic things get said.

If, as my clients do, we attempt to create and put our creative work—our novels, paintings, scientific theories, inventions, business ideas—out into the world for everyone to see, then our peers and our friends become our natural critics. Because these creations mean so much to us, because so much of our efforts at meaning making goes into them, criticism of our creative work hurts like nothing else—and can rupture relationships. That almost happened in the following instance:

Dear Gail,

You are a good friend, and you know me as well as anyone, but when you laughed at one of my haiku and said I should find another pursuit, it hurt like a slap in the face. I pretty much stopped writing them after that, and the few that I write I never show to anyone. I'd found a writing endeavor that I enjoyed, and though I realized I wasn't a great writer, I thought some of them were worth sharing. As you also said, I probably should have stuck with being a visual artist. I'm just a person with not much talent for words. Poor me.

Your friend,
Violet

We do not expect our acquaintances to mind our interests and our feelings as well as our friends should. Nevertheless we are frequently blindsided and hurt by what our peers have to say, especially when that criticism comes in a writers' or painters' "critique group" when we are feeling particularly vulnerable. At such times, when group members have implicit permission to be as critical as they like, they often cross the line into cruelty under the cover of "giving constructive feedback." Here is a typical story:

Dear Critique Group Partners:

I am writing you from Yugoslavia. I hope your club is as active as it was in the past, with interesting people and interesting writing. Yet I must say to you now that some of your criticism was too harsh, too unjust. Too many times you tore my texts to pieces. Sometimes I was so demoralized that I was afraid of reading in public, and I took a long time until I dared write again. I know that I am not the only one with this experience in this group. It doesn't matter if this is the general way with literary criticism. Something bad does not become good just because it is the custom of the trade or repeated many times.

And my texts were OK. Not only OK—they were good. I received quite different feedback from other people, such as when I recently read one of my short stories at a literary evening. The folks there took an intuitive approach and not a dissecting approach. When you dissect a living thing, you kill it. You almost killed my literary impulses. Fortunately they rose up again, and now I am a published and award-winning writer. My readers love my texts precisely for the reason you rejected them: because they are written from the heart.

Anyway, I didn't want to insult you, and I know you didn't want to insult me either. But sometimes your way of communicating was insulting. Yes, your parties were the greatest parties of my life! But I do think you should do less "criticism," which has as its Greek root "cutting," and more life-giving nourishment. You should feed the people in your group more and hurt them less. Those are my feelings.

With greetings,
Sonya

Working the Six Keys with Critical Friends

Criticism from friends and peers is an unavoidable feature of life. It is made more unavoidable if the work you do opens you up to criticism. You deal with this unavoidable criticism in the same way that you deal with all criticism, by mindfully working the six keys. Here is an example of that mindful work.

Max is a sculptor who recently turned sixty. His best friend, Paul, is a painter who stopped painting two years back and recently began dabbling in sculpture. Paul is able to dabble because he has a working wife who supports him and because he has built up an inventory of paintings and prints of his paintings that continue to sell, though only sporadically.

Recently Paul has begun to criticize Max for not playing more, now that they are both sixty and "old enough to be retired," for not trying out the drugs that have made their way back into Paul's life ("Do you even *remember* what getting high felt like?"), and, most toxically, for complaining that sculpture isn't really an artistic endeavor, that it's "like manufacturing, like making a sink or a table." Max has been able to laugh all this off so far, but he is beginning to suspect that if Paul continues knocking the meaning of sculpture, he may yet provoke a meaning crisis in Max.

A precipitating crisis arrives. Paul comes over to Max's studio just as Max is having his own doubts about the sculpture in front of him, a life-size human figure made of brightly painted plaster of paris. Paul wanders in and exclaims, "Yeah, you know you're stuck when you need to paint your sculptures! I told you that sculpture wasn't strong enough by itself!" Max, suddenly furious, finds an excuse to send Paul packing and makes up his mind that something must be done.

Later that day he sits down and writes out his thoughts, using the six keys as a template:

> The existential key: Even if I have rocky days and even if I have my existential doubts and crises, I know that I make my meaning by sculpting. Paul is in a new state (or maybe this is just a new phase of the state he has always been in) and doesn't know where to make his meaning, so he wants to play, to distract himself, and feels the need to knock sculpture, maybe because he's predicting that he will never be good enough to satisfy himself in that medium. This return to drugs is the clearest indication of the meaning crisis overtaking him. So, given that he is in the middle of a meaning crisis and I am not (yet, anyway!), what am I supposed to do? Be compassionate? Help him? Or stay the hell out of his way while he implodes or explodes or whatever?
>
> This leads me right to the appraisal key, I guess. If I'm honest about it, the truth is that I'm worried myself about these new sculp-

tures and worried that Paul's criticism has a ring of truth. Why did I move from stone to painted plaster of paris? Well, I can articulate the reasons, but I also have my doubts. But—but doubt isn't a problem! Doubt has never been a problem before. Of course an artist has doubts. Paul is doing something different from doubting; he is giving up, disrespecting the nature of the journey and the nature of the task. So, what should I conclude? I must conclude that, despite our thirty years of friendship, I must be very careful of where Paul is today. He is not in a good place for me. That doesn't mean I have to "fire" him as a friend—but I do have to do something.

Max's bottom-line conclusion is that Paul is a danger to him right now. Paul's criticisms of the meaningfulness of sculpture and his late-life meaning crisis put Max at risk for his own meaning derailment. Although the odds of that meaning derailment are long, they are real, and Max decides to quietly cut Paul off. He takes a longer time than before to answer Paul's e-mails; when he does answer them, his answers are on the terse side; he avoids inviting Paul to the studio. To Max, this doesn't signal the end of their friendship, but it does constitute something of a temporary separation.

Max recognizes that he could take another approach: that of being a good friend to Paul and helping him through this crisis. In thinking about it, however, Max realizes that Paul's crisis has spanned their thirty years of friendship, that for all those years Paul has worked too little, too superficially, and in a grandiose, querulous way that, even if rooted in self-doubt, played itself out as criticism of those around him—Max usually excepted. This crisis is not new and not even worse than some of Paul's previous ones. Therefore, it would be folly to suppose there was a way he could help Paul—except, of course, by holding himself available to be beaten up, existentially speaking. Max can't see the sense in that. For a period of time he keeps Paul at arm's length.

It would be nice if there were a cookie-cutter way to respond to all criticism, maybe by ignoring it or by always replying "Never say that to me again!" But there is no one-size-fits-all response. Each time you are criticized, you find yourself in a unique situation that requires mindful attention. Many times you will be able to brush the criticism aside as irrelevant, and in that sense becoming the sort of person who is good at "brushing criticism aside" is the closest you can come to possessing an all-purpose response to criticism. But even if you become expert at brushing most criticism aside, you have to appraise whether a given criticism is of that sort. You have to be mindful even then.

This is especially true when it comes to friends. Every friendship is a provisional relationship, kept alive because it has value and worth, not because it is abstractly sanctified. A good friendship will survive irritations and even crises, but its contours—and very life—must be judged according to its reality. You may have excellent reasons to stand behind a friend who is critical of you—or you may not. When a friend criticizes you, you do not need to stuff your reaction, so as to spare your friend's feelings, or to feel hurt and betrayed, never supposing that a friend would criticize you. You simply need to be mindful, work the six keys, and make sense of this particular criticism and this particular friendship.

Working the Six Keys with Critical Peers

At twenty-six, Maya is a third-year doctoral student in anthropology at a large, prestigious university. Her peers are quick-witted, competitive, ambitious, critical graduate students, each of whom has an investment in rising to the top of the graduate pool, making the most contacts, publishing the most articles, and getting the most funding. Much of the criticism is of the behind-the-back sort, as on the surface the graduate students in Maya's department are cordial, helpful, and supportive of one another. But when any two gather, a third is raked over the coals.

One of the places where this criticism manifests itself publicly is in dissertation seminar, which Maya is currently taking. It is the stated objective of the class that students in the class critique each other's dissertation proposals, which mandate provides permission and cover for unbridled criticizing. This week Maya presented her proposal for a comparative study of two urban subcultures in San Francisco and, although anticipating criticism, never expected the all-out assault her proposal received from two fourth-years, Joyce and Phillip. Her first reaction was to doubt her proposal, to doubt herself, to fantasize fleeing the graduate-school environment, and to hide under the covers. Her second reaction was to deal with this barrage of criticism mindfully, employing the six keys.

First she asks herself if anything about this criticism has changed her mind about her life path. Is she suddenly less interested in becoming a professor because of the attack on her dissertation proposal? Maya treats this as a real question, not a rhetorical one, and spends some time thinking through whether the doubts she has always harbored about a life in academia have crystallized because of this criticism and tipped her toward a new path. She pictures in her mind's eye other lives, as a lawyer, as a writer, in the nonprofit world, in the corporate world, running her own business, becoming a translator (because of her love for Italian), raising children as a stay-at-home mom. She thinks through the pros and cons of each path, trying as best she can to do an honorable job of weighing, and in the end concludes that no life allows her as much freedom or provides as good a container for meaning as that of university professor.

Maya is pleasantly surprised to discover that the sting of the criticism leveled at her by Joyce and Phillip has eased tremendously by virtue of her reaffirming her commitment to her present path. Their criticisms now seem more like pinpricks than bomb blasts. She finds herself suddenly equal to appraising the actual merits of their criticism. Joyce called her proposal "so far on the qualitative side as to rival fiction." Phillip argued that her hypothesis contained terms that couldn't be defined operationally, thereby rendering her proposal meaningless. Maya considers these objections.

Because of her firm belief that the social sciences have more in common with the humanities than with the hard sciences, the conceits of social scientists notwithstanding, she finds herself completely untroubled by the possibility that her project isn't "hard science" enough for the likes of Joyce and Phillip. The only question is whether her thesis advisers will accept its "softness." Her primary adviser already looks to be on board, and Maya has the sense that she can find two other faculty members in the "soft camp" who will accept the descriptive, qualitative nature of her dissertation. She suddenly realizes that she has come up with a working principle: criticism of her proposal by her thesis advisers will matter; criticism of it by her peers will not.

Maya now asks herself, "What sort of attitude do I want to adopt with Joyce, Phillip, and the others?" She gives this some thought and decides she would like to be "bigger than them" and treat them decently and compassionately, even if they can't or won't return the favor. At the same time she decides she would like to remain completely indifferent to them, taking a sort of "friendly stonewall" position with her graduate-school peers, not revealing much to them, not confiding much in them, and especially not gossiping much with them. Her mantra becomes "kind, helpful, but very careful." Both the sting and the importance of the criticism she received in class recede in light of this attitude adjustment.

Next Maya wonders whether anything in her self-talk or personality contributed to the toxicity of the moment. It becomes clear to her as she thinks about it that certain doubts about whether she is good enough and smart enough to excel at this level, and certain simmering conflicts about whether she chose the right adviser, the right university, and the right academic field were activated by Joyce's and Phillip's remarks. It occurs to her that to prevent criticism about her research from triggering crises, she needs to have an affirmation or warning handy. She tries out several and finally lands on the following: "I will not take criticism of my research as an opportunity to reevaluate my whole life!" This she reduces to the simpler "No mountains out of molehills!"

Finally Maya asks herself, "What behaviors go with this decision to ignore the peer criticism I receive during graduate school?" After thinking the matter over, she comes to the following conclusions: that whenever someone criticizes her research methodology, she is going to respond with "Let me think about that"; and that, when she asks for feedback on her projects, which she will sometimes have to do, she will carefully delineate the kind of feedback she wants, so as to disallow a criticism "open-door policy."

Minimizing Toxic Criticism from Friends and Peers

The first step in minimizing toxic criticism is always the same: becoming a person who finds most criticism existentially irrelevant and therefore easy to ignore. Other tasks include accurately

appraising the situation, adopting a phlegmatic and philosophical attitude, getting a grip on your mind and taking charge of
your self-talk, and so on. When it is a friend who criticizes you,
however, the whole weight and history of the friendship also
become part of the appraisal process.

We balance a history of loyalty against a single rude remark.
Conversely, we count a single jab as a real body blow if it follows
a long history of jabs. With friends, the contextual nature of the
current criticism is crucial, as what we are really weighing is the
value of the friendship. We may decide that with someone else
we would air our grievance, but we are going to let this friend
slide, because of her current situation. We may decide that our
friend's critical remark is something much more disturbing than
mere criticism: that it represents a profound lack of respect,
which implies that we lack sufficient self-respect.

Peers also hold a special place in our life. We measure our success in the world and on the job against them; we interact with
them as equals and often as competitors; we look to them to val-
idate our efforts and provide us with feedback. With peers it is a
reasonable policy to react to their criticism with the inner warning "It may be because of their agenda." Because we are their
competitors, too, because we stand in the same provocative relationship to them that they stand to us, it makes sense that their
objectivity will often be clouded by their agenda.

Our friends and our peers are likely to be our own age, share
our interests and opinions, hang out where we hang out, read
what we read, see the same movies, listen to the same music—in
short, be very much like us. As such, they have special power to
get under our skin and into our head when they criticize us. We
guard against this in all the ways I've been describing and in the
following additional way: by regularly reminding ourselves that
criticism need not feel more poignant or more painful because
the person delivering it is an intimate or an associate.

To consider

- What are some of the special difficulties in dealing with criticism from friends?
- To which of the six keys (existential, appraisal, attitudinal, cognitive, personality, or behavioral) do you need to pay the most attention when the criticism you receive is "friendly fire"?
- What are some of the special difficulties in dealing with criticism from peers?
- To which of the six keys do you need to pay the most attention when the criticism you receive is from a peer?

To do

- If a rupture over criticism has recently occurred in one of your friendships, think through what you would like to do about it—and then do it.
- If a rupture over criticism has recently occurred in one of your peer relationships, think through what you would like to do about it—and then do it.

9

Criticism in the Workplace

Work comes with criticism attached. Workplace criticism may come from your boss, from your coworkers, from clients or customers. There is no spot so high or so low on the work food chain that it immunizes you from criticism. Indeed, hardly a day goes by in most work environments that something that feels like criticism doesn't come your way, whether it's a brusque e-mail from a colleague or an unreturned phone call from a prospect, a sideways glance from a manager or a generic office memo complaining about trash in the break room.

Four Toxic Work Challenges

Because work environments can be routinely toxic, out of necessity people come up with ways of coping. Many of these are of the ineffective sort that we discussed at the beginning of the book. These range from pill popping and luncheon drinking to stuffing the criticism and eventually getting ill to acting out passive-aggressively. Indeed, people often deal more ineffectively with work criticism than with other criticism, because of the special challenges that exist in the workplace. Among these special challenges are the following four.

Strategic, Not Intimate

On balance, relationships at work are *strategic* and not intimate. The kind of heartfelt truth-telling that might be appropriate, useful, and beneficial with friends, family members, and loved ones may be inappropriate, counterproductive, and even disastrous in a work setting. As a rule, work is a place for strategizing, not soul bearing. In a work setting, the main challenge is to deal with criticism strategically.

Systemic, Not Personal

A considerable amount of the criticism that comes your way at work is *systemic* and not personal. It arises because of the nature of the system in which you find yourself and the role you play in that system. If you hand out parking summonses or answer customer complaints, your role provokes angry criticism as a matter of course. If it's your job to keep the library quiet, turn down loans, or investigate malfeasance, it comes with a built-in criticism quotient that has nothing to do with you as a person. If you make and sell a product, your competitors may feel obliged to criticize it (and you) even if they themselves use your product. If your job comes with an evaluation process, along comes criticism. Virtually every job has these built-in pockets of criticism.

Part of an Agenda

It can be especially hard to make sense of the criticism you receive at work because of the many agendas swirling around you. You may have little or no idea what pressure your boss is under, such as to increase productivity or to serve the bottom line, and that it's those pressures and nothing about you that cause him to criticize you about how long your project took or what your project cost. Nor is it easy to judge which criticism we can routinely ignore and which we are supposed to take to heart, as not heeding someone's pet peeve—for instance, that we are wasting copy paper—may prove more damaging than not heeding some seemingly more important criticism. In these regards work is as much a mystery as it is a minefield.

Asking Coworkers to Help Interpret Criticism

It can prove dangerous to enlist others to help you *make sense* of the criticism you receive at work, as your coworkers have their own agendas and may turn what you say to their own use and advantage. This means that, at least until you get home and can talk the matter over with your partner or a good friend, you are obliged to maintain a certain silence, which can easily turn into a brooding silence as you stew about the criticism you just received. Some of the most dramatic outbursts at work come at the end of the day, after a person has sat with a criticism all day long without a good way to vent her feelings or get some counsel. This necessary stonewalling *self-counsel* is another special challenge of the work environment.

These four challenges—the need to be strategic, the systemic nature of much workplace criticism, the challenge of making sense of the criticism, and the need to opt for silence and self-counsel—lead us to our headline "first response" to workplace criticism. Rather than reacting at all, you get a grip on your mind, your personality, and your emotions and tell yourself in no uncertain terms, "Let me think about this."

Why It's Crucial to Give Yourself Time to Reflect

A poignant challenge of dealing with criticism at work is that when a criticism comes at you from out of the blue it can feel like an attack, and we are wired to fight or flee in the face of attacks.

Fleeing to the bathroom to gather yourself is no particular problem, but fighting back—counterattacking—can damage your relationship with a coworker or boss and even endanger your career. Rather than counterattacking, your best bet is to instantly switch the internal message from "I'm being attacked!" to "Let me think about this." You go from heightened affect and drama to stillness and a near-meditative state by getting a grip on your mind and changing your internal message.

The attack can feel doubly hard to handle if it contains hot-button slurs that instantly rile you. It is bad enough to be told that you are doing a bad job. It is worse if the criticism is followed up with a muttered "Never would have happened except for affirmative action." Your face may flush and your palms may begin to sweat if your boss drops the bombshell "You are really not working up to your potential." Your temperature may rise another few degrees, however, if your boss adds, "And to think we bent over backward with your maternity leave." This piling on of criticism, as it were, which is likely to trigger the desire to defend yourself and counterattack, is still best met with mental self-control and the internal mantra "Let me think about this."

Use the "Dear Critic" Letters

When you get home—possibly still steaming—you can process the incident and write a "Dear critic" letter that allows you to vent, get clear on what happened, and plot your course of action. Here is one such "Dear critic" letter, from Suzanne:

Dear Frank:

People love the opportunity to improve themselves, but how we respond to criticism depends on how it is offered. I personally respond very well when someone suggests ways to improve, but not when it starts with an attack on how I am now. Unless what I was doing was just plain awful, such an attack is unwarranted—unless you had previously gently requested that I change, which you did not do in this case. The first mention of how I conduct myself at meetings came in our latest meeting, where you blasted me and suggested that my ego made it essential that I always come up with the right answer and not let anyone else do it. You continued with an observation that I didn't act the way your wife did, which implied (to me) that your wife was a paragon of business behavior and that all should follow—at least, all women should follow—this lead.

My first comment is that I doubt you would have said any of the above to your male employees. Being assertive in a meeting is an asset—in some way, I think you expressed more of your own limitations regarding sexual equality in this discussion than any failure in business protocol on mine. Second, the meeting in question (and others referenced) was designed solely to solve a given problem. As everyone's time is valuable, the idea is to come up with a bunch of solutions and then pick the best, as quickly as possible. I see no value in holding back my thoughts to allow others to think of the same thing, just to satisfy some ego need of theirs.

If, after reading this, you still feel you have a comment to make, please share it with me, or it might be better to have a moderated meeting, perhaps with an HR person, to make sure an independent person is able to mediate this discussion. You know, I think that's what's needed here: a mediated meeting with an HR person. Let me get back to you on whether I want to do that, as I know that probably escalates matters. Hmm . . . I wonder what your wife would do.

Thrilled not to be your wife,
Suzanne

Dealing with a Bad Performance Review

Whether Suzanne sets up the mediated meeting with HR or not, confronts her boss or says nothing, or stays at or leaves her job, she will at least have given herself the time to think through how she wants to proceed, by not reacting in the moment and by reminding herself to think rather than feel. Consider a second example, a "Dear critic" letter written after an unexpectedly negative performance review:

Dear Mel:

You recently presented me with my performance review. First, I believe it would have been more effective had I known earlier of your concerns, so I would have had an opportunity to correct them. I felt broadsided by the extent and scope of your criticism. Most of these were issues that could easily have been mentioned during the quarter; having heard nothing until now, I felt it was reasonable to assume I was doing well. Second, I tend to disagree with some of your conclusions. You have suggested that I wasn't aggressive enough in trying to generate sales, but in fact, as I am not the sales rep, all I was supposed to do was to help them become aware of opportunities I had seen; I cannot close deals. Though I frequently mentioned my efforts, and the failure of the reps to pursue them, you apparently didn't consider this enough of an effort. But you also failed to explain that to me.

I accept that I may not have been your star performer, but I believe that the manager-employee relationship involves teamwork and communication. If I did poorly, in your view, at least part of this has to be attributed to poor communication on your part. How can I know what you expect or how you rate my performance if there is no ongoing discussion? I realize criticism isn't fun for either of us, but then, it is critical in achieving our goals. I feel my review should be reconsidered based on the fact that I did the best I could do, given the information provided to me.

Yours,
Dianne

Dianne, like Suzanne, is in the hard position of learning that she is not that well liked by her boss and that her work life is in some jeopardy. She can't make these facts go away by waving a magic wand. What she can do—and what is in her best interests to do—is to stop herself from reacting in the moment to the critical comments fired her way and give herself the chance to think through what the criticism actually means and how she wants to proceed. When you are criticized at work, internally reacting with "Let me think about this" is your best approach.

Ten Communication Tips to Use at Work

A real part of the challenge of handling criticism at work is in understanding what the criticism means. Was it meant in jest or in earnest? Was it personal or role specific? Was it offhanded or long simmering? By becoming a communications expert at work, you increase your chances of gaining the information you need to put each criticism in its rightful place. Follow these ten tips to become a better communicator at work:

1. **Don't treat work communications cavalierly**. Every message you send at work provides information about you as a worker, a team player, a potential leader, or a potential problem. Every message you receive reveals aspects of your work environment and informs you about your fellow workers. Messages at work are always significant: they reveal who you are and educate you about your fellow workers.

2. **Respond to messages at work in a calculated way.** Even if we have only a split second to process a message and respond, we want to calculate our response. We are excellent calculating machines and can do a good job quickly. If you can't decide how to proceed, then pause and say, "Let me think about that. I'll get

back to you first thing this afternoon." Give yourself the time you need to calculate your response.

3. **Get brilliant about hidden agendas.** How can you tell what someone means by her message? Experience is the guide. When you deal with a person for a while, you get a sense of what her messages mean. Given this person, what do her words probably mean? Given their probable meaning, how do you want to reply? Remember to reply to the meaning in a message, not to the words.

4. **If you can't decode an important message, ask for clarification.** Often we have to guess at the meaning of a message, because it is impractical to ask for clarification every time some message confuses us. But when a message feels important and we can't decode it, then asking for clarification is a sensible option. Remember, an unclear message stays unclear until you get clarification from the person who sent it.

5. **Know that you've been heard by checking in and asking questions.** If we need to get our message across and we aren't sure we have, then we need to muster the courage to ask follow-up questions and make sure our message got delivered. You may feel embarrassed and fear looking foolish when, for instance, you admit that the message you sent may not have been clear, but it is worth a little embarrassment to be understood. If you think your message hasn't been heard, it probably hasn't.

6. **Don't let your nerves stop you from getting the information you need or from saying what you need to say.** Have you said nothing about your workload doubling? Have you wanted to try your hand at a new challenge but not gotten around to asking your supervisor for permission? Have a quiet conversation with yourself and calm yourself down. Tell yourself that you needn't be frightened. Prepare what you want to say— and then say it. Fear can be a gift—or a curse. Don't let your nerves silence you unnecessarily.

7. **When warning bells go off, hold your tongue.** Practically nothing makes us more miserable and causes us more trouble than saying something that, an instant later, we wish we hadn't said. Not only do we risk harming our work relationships, but we risk wasting inordinate time obsessing about the mistake we made and trying to figure out how to patch things up. Sometimes we need to speak when we don't really want to. Sometimes we need not to speak when we do want to.

8. **Gossip carefully.** Adding to office gossip can come back to haunt us. It also doesn't feel very principled. We feel our smallest, sneakiest, meanest, and cattiest when we gossip. Part of us enjoys it, but another part—the better part—recognizes that we are indulging some primitive urge and not living up to our highest standards. Gossip a little—it's only natural. But gossip carefully and keep it to a minimum.

9. **Be clear about your motivation before you speak.** You can do yourself great harm by not knowing what is really motivating your speech. If you don't know why you are speaking, you don't know what you are saying. Usually we would know why we intended to say something if only we had stopped for a count of ten and asked ourselves the question "What's going on here?" As soon as we ask that question, we invite ourselves to enter into fruitful inner dialogue and identify any covert motivation that is secretly driving us.

10. **Be smart when you do the criticizing.** Anytime we have to tell people that they need to do something differently or that they've done something wrong, we are criticizing them. You will almost certainly have to do some criticizing in your work life. How you criticize is up to you. You can use the moment to vent, to get a dig in, to let general negative feelings about work infect your message, to let your anger about something else leak into your evaluation, or to publicly ridicule someone. Or you can get a grip on your mind and your personality and criticize carefully.

Artful Criticizing in the Workplace

Offering artful criticism in the workplace requires thought and effort but pays off in the end. Because of the care you take, there will be fewer ruptures to repair and fewer interpersonal fires to put out. Here are some examples of workplace criticism, from worst to best:

- Pure venting: "This report is a piece of garbage! You're an idiot!"
- Genteel venting, with a dig intended: "You didn't do a very good job on this report. What were you thinking?"
- Direct criticism, unadorned but also unhelpful: "This report doesn't work."
- Separating the person from the product and starting with a positive: "You're usually terrific at this, but this report doesn't work."
- Separating the person from the product, starting with a positive, and also providing guidance: "You're usually terrific at this, but this report doesn't work. I need you to revise the last part, where you make your recommendations without explaining how they would help us meet our budget concerns."

You can make use of these ten communication tips, and other communication improvements that you institute, as part of your larger program of working the six keys. Try out at least one of these communication tips as soon as you can.

Work the Six Keys

Sarah, a shy twenty-seven-year-old, teaches English and history at a middle school. In the middle of her third year of teaching, she can now manage a classroom well enough that the work of teaching (as opposed to the work of maintaining order) gets done. Her main problem is her relationship with the school's principal, Betty, who came to the school the year after Sarah arrived. It seems to Sarah that whenever Betty catches sight of her she immediately begins frowning. Sarah is pretty certain she isn't being paranoid, as Betty's frowns are right in line with the evaluations that Betty has offered after each of her three class-room visits. The evaluations were on balance positive, but each ended with the following criticism: "Your students can't hear you!" On the third evaluation, this comment came with three exclamation points attached.

Sarah is coming up for a spring salary talk and is dreading meeting with Betty. To prepare for the meeting, Sarah decides to work the six keys. As she thinks about the first key, the existen-tial key, she realizes that she doesn't want her teaching career jeopardized by this principal, and that criticism from any princi-pal, even one who may not be objective and who may have taken a dislike to her, shouldn't be ignored. Sarah accepts that she must assess the situation mindfully and thoroughly, as it matters to her that she continue teaching.

Next she tackles the second key, that of trying to appraise the situation. The first question that arises is the following one: "When Betty says that my students can't hear me, am I to take that literally, or is that a metaphor?" Sarah spends a whole Satur-day morning wondering about this question as she goes about her business of running errands and doing chores. At noon it strikes her what Betty's complaint is really all about. Betty doesn't admire diffident people; she regularly says to students and teachers alike, "Don't hide your light under a barrel!" Betty is actually demand-ing that Sarah act more confidently in the classroom. For Betty, speaking up must be a behavioral indicator of confidence. Betty wants to see a more assertive, forceful Sarah in the classroom.

Sarah finds herself nodding. That feels like exactly the right analysis of the situation. Betty isn't down on Sarah as much as she is upset at the gap between Sarah's teaching persona and some ideal teaching persona that Betty has in mind for all teachers. Sarah has the sense that she can skip right to the sixth key, to the behavioral key, because what is required of her, she suddenly realizes, is a change in the following direction: she must act more confidently in the classroom. Even if her natural inclination is toward quiet diffidence, she has been put on notice by her principal that diffidence is out and forcefulness is in.

She spends the rest of that Saturday pondering how to make such a change (in essence working the third, fourth, and fifth keys). Several ideas pop into her head. She could join Toastmasters and become a more accomplished and less nervous public speaker. She could try her hand at community theater, toward the same end. She could take a confidence-building workshop; she sees advertisements for such workshops all the time. She could do a one-on-one sort of thing, perhaps working with a voice teacher on her actual voice or with a life coach on building confidence. By that Saturday night she has created a long list of possibilities, and by Sunday morning, having slept on it, she has made up her mind.

By Monday afternoon Sarah has researched her options and made her commitments. On Tuesday morning she sends Betty the following e-mail:

Dear Betty:

I wanted to let you know what steps I'm taking to meet your concerns about my classroom demeanor. I've never been very good at (or, truth be told, very concerned about) projecting my voice, but I recognize that I need to get better at that, so I will begin on Thursday working regularly with a voice teacher on voice projection. And to help me grow more confident in the classroom, I've decided to take a series of weekend seminars offered through that institute you mentioned last year at a faculty meeting. Thanks for your feedback. I feel confident that these new efforts will pay off in the classroom!

Best,
Sarah

Not ten minutes later Sarah receives a return e-mail: "Hi, Sarah: Sounds great! And I look forward to our salary chat next week—Betty."

Sarah finds herself smiling. She knows that she's reacted strategically and smartly to what may have been a fair or—who knows? —an unfair criticism of her classroom performance. Now, instead of dreading her meeting with Betty, she discovers she is actually looking forward to it.

When You Work in the Arts

My creativity coaching clients are in the arts and work in environments like dance companies, bands, symphony orchestras, theater ensembles, or, most usually, in the solitude of their studio or study where they write, paint, or compose and from which they send their work out into the world.

Much of the criticism they receive is of the following sort: they or their products are not wanted. They feel criticized by virtue of not landing a part, not hearing back from editors about their latest short story, not getting any response from gallery owners to their e-mail inquiries, not making any sales during open studio weekends. People in the arts must deal with these and other special challenges, among them all of the following:

• An artist is always selling and must weather the built-in criticism that comes with a sales job. Between 90 percent and 98 percent of the time what he is selling won't be wanted, so between 90 percent and 98 percent of the time he has the opportunity to feel criticized. Even a well-attended gallery event that produces a number of sales can be construed by the artist as a critical failure: "Of the two hundred people who came, only three liked me!" A lifetime of selling equals a lifetime of criticism, if (and only if) an artist holds each no-sale as criticism.

• An artist automatically sets himself up to be judged and compared against the best in his field by virtue of doing nothing more than his work. A lawyer who writes a will doesn't have to hear from his client, "John in Dallas writes a much better will!" But every artist gets to hear, in one form or another, sometimes directly and sometimes indirectly, sometimes gently and sometimes rudely, "You are no Pavarotti!" or "You are no Shakespeare!" This judging and comparing goes on for as long as an artist persists in working—and even after he stops working—and even after he is dead.

• With success come new challenges and new opportunities for criticism. A writer who finally has a book published, after a decade of the implied criticism that attaches to not getting published, now faces tasks for which she is entirely unprepared, like fielding radio interviews or answering questions at book signings. A studio artist who may have had little contact with the world is now suddenly presumed to be equal to performance challenges like national media engagements.

Here is a poignant "Dear critic" letter from one such writer, written after a difficult book-signing event. Janine wrote:

Dear Ms. Book Tour Organizer:

Thank you for your efforts in organizing last weekend's reading. While the discussion with the audience seemed to elicit a positive response, I felt by your comments to me after the event that you were not pleased with my lack of spontaneity in presenting my story and in answering the questions of the audience. Perhaps I was remiss in not telling you ahead of time that when in a situation such as last Saturday, with many people, lights, and microphones, I tend to become overwhelmed by the stimulation and am not able to prevent my automatic defense mechanism from kicking in to prevent what it thinks is a deadly assault.

As you know from my writing, I do indeed have much to say and want to continue to work with you in any way necessary to help sell my book. When planning the next presentation, I would love the opportunity to have more input regarding the placement of the podium—i.e., without the light from the window shining in my eyes —and in a place in the room where I am not feeling trapped in the corner. As I mentioned to you, the people walking around were a great distraction to me. I don't know that there will always be a solution to that problem, but in the future I will make every effort to arrive well in advance of the starting time so that I have time to familiarize myself with the space and its ambience.

Thank you again for your efforts,
Janine

A second example is a "Dear critic" letter written by a non-fiction writer who thought it wise to create a teleclass to help publicize her just-published self-help book. She then had to deal with the criticism that often accompanies first-time attempts at anything. Rachel wrote:

Dear Mary,

Thank you for your recent e-mail about the teleclass last week. I appreciate feedback because my goal is to help as many people as I can move from the pain of loss to keeping the loving memories alive. I know that it isn't possible to provide something that works for every single person, but if there is something that I can do to improve the format of the class, I would like to know more about it. Would you mind helping me out by answering a few questions in addition to the comments that you already provided?

When you read the class description, what is it you expected to get from the class? Which of those expectations were met? How? Which of those expectations were not met? What would need to happen differently in the class for them to be met? What would you need to do differently for them to be met? Do you have any other ideas for improving the class?

Thanks again, Mary, for writing. I have enclosed a coupon for you if you would like to attend the next offering of this class or any of my other ones as my personal guest.

Sincerely,
Rachel

The second you jot down your first poem, sketch your first comic strip, audition for your first school play, or take your first clarinet lesson, you announce to the world "It is open season! You may start criticizing me!" All artists face the same painful challenge, which is only an exaggerated version of the challenge we all face as soon as we put ourselves out for hire: that criticism is a built-in feature of every work environment.

To consider

- What do you see as some of the special challenges of handling criticism in your line of work?
- What can you do to better deal with these challenges?

- What do you see as some of the special challenges of handling criticism where you currently work?
- What can you do to deal better with these challenges?

To do

- Think through a time when you were criticized at work. Get the situation clearly in mind and then "redo" the situation working the six keys. Learn from this exercise how you intend to handle criticism at work the next time it occurs.

10

Other Varieties of Criticism We Commonly Face

In this chapter we'll explore four varieties of criticism: indirect and implied criticism, criticism from experts and critics, criticism of your group, and criticism from strangers. Taken together with the varieties of criticism we've already explored—criticism from family members, loved ones, friends, and peers; criticism at work; and self-criticism—this will complete our exploration of the kinds of criticism we regularly face.

Indirect and Implied Criticism: A Challenge to Deal With

A lot of the criticism we receive is indirect or implied. Your mother buys your younger sister a blouse but doesn't buy you one, implying that she is the pretty one and you are the plain one. Your brother is ferried to all of his baseball practices, but you have to a catch a ride with the parents of your friends to get to your soccer practices, indirectly announcing which child is held in higher esteem or at least seen as the athlete in the family. Your boss gives your coworker a complicated assignment that he might just as easily have given to you, implying that you can't handle something that complex. At home, at work, and in every facet of daily life, we find ourselves confronted by indirect criticism and implied criticism.

John recalled that in his family direct criticism was forbidden. As everyone in the family had a critical nature and couldn't function without criticizing someone or something, family members had to find covert and discreet ways of criticizing one another. John learned that he could criticize his fundamentalist parents by maintaining friends of various faiths and dabbling in esoteric religions. They, in turn, would criticize his ecumenical spirit indirectly, by holding dinner table conversations about the blood sacrifices of the Incas and the real estate holdings of the Roman Catholic Church. He never took their bait, and so all you saw were two parents chatting amiably and three teenagers eating and minding their business. Yet this environment could not have been more poisonous. In the end, John's older sister, Marcia, had to be hospitalized for anorexia and his younger sister, Alison, committed suicide between her freshman and sophomore years at college. These disasters made no sense to friends and family, who had never heard a harsh word uttered in that household.

Susan, by contrast, grew up in an angry household where the criticism was as overt as the anger. Still, she was tormented by implied and indirect criticism that proved equally cruel and damaging. Her mother railed at her directly for her eating habits and her chubbiness but managed to double that criticism by sending her to her room when company arrived, on the grounds that there weren't enough snacks for everyone, implying that she would make a pig of herself. Or she would buy Susan only the dowdiest clothes, implying that she had no shot at being of interest to boys.

If Susan complained about the clothes her mother bought for her, her mother would reply, "That's all we can afford!" This was almost worse than her mother replying frankly, "This is all you deserve, considering how you look." If Susan complained about

being sent to her room when company arrived and even humiliated herself by pledging not to touch the crackers and cheese, her
mother's "Just do your homework!" was almost worse than a direct
"I don't trust you not to embarrass us by wolfing down the snacks."

Indirect criticism and implied criticism look like all of the
following:

- You are Mexican-American, and as he watches you work,
  your boss mutters, "This town has gotten very brown."
- Instead of saying that your lips are too thin for current filmic
  taste, your agent tells you that the director is looking for an
  "Angelina Jolie type."
- At Thanksgiving dinner at your parents' house, you are
  seated at the second table with the neighbors from down
  the block rather than at the main table.
- Your mate, who has been at you for the way the house looks,
  buys you a carpet sweeper as your anniversary present.
- You've left early all week, and on Friday afternoon your
  coworker innocently asks, "Will you have time to work on
  our project before you leave today?"

Exactly because it is indirect and implied rather than direct
and explicit, criticism of this sort is among the most difficult to
handle. Often you feel completely at sea, unable to judge whether
you have been criticized, unable to decide whether the person
delivering the criticism is being offhanded or calculating, unable
to find a way to process the criticism or vent your feelings. There
even seems to be a kind of implicit contract in place: "Yes, I criticized you, but I didn't say anything to give you real offense, so
you can't really call me on anything I said, because that would
blow the whole thing out of proportion—haha! And I can always
say you misunderstood! Won't you look foolish then? So you have
no choice but to remain silent; that's the deal."

It isn't. There is no such social contract in place unless you accept its existence. You can say to your coworker, "I know I've been leaving early this week, but I have my reasons. Today, as it happens, I'll be around until six." You can say to your mate, "I think you're trying to tell me something about the way the house looks with this carpet sweeper. If that's the case, we need to have a chat. If you meant nothing by it, then all I can say is I would have preferred jewelry." You can say to your mom, "What were you thinking when you seated me with the neighbors and not the family? I'm really curious." You can be direct and explicit, if you decide that being direct and explicit serves you, even as those around you are being coy, cruel, and passive-aggressive.

Criticism from Experts and Critics

Every field, walk of life, and culture has its experts and professional critics. There are military experts, religious experts, medical experts, legal experts. The village shaman feels empowered to approve of certain practices and denounce other practices; the art critic feels empowered to approve of certain art and denounce other art; the high school English teacher feels empowered to grade students and rank some as superior and some as failures.

If something can be rated—whether it's a restaurant, hotel, movie, CD, or city—it will be. Someone will step forward to announce how subjects should be handled in social science experiments, how poems should be ranked in a contest, who should be judged mad, and even how the birth of the universe should be construed. Criticism from self-styled experts and critics is ubiquitous. If you work in the arts, as my clients do, it is part of your landscape from the moment your preschool teacher pronounces your blue sun wrong.

What does criticism from experts and critics feel like? Consider this "Dear critic" letter from Allen, a comic:

Dear Critic,

I observed you during my performance. You scowled the whole time, shaking your head, rolling your eyes, and sighing loudly. Or else you had a blank look on your face while almost everyone else was laughing. After the show, you were overheard in the lobby saying "I'm glad I didn't have to pay for that."

A few days later your review appeared. I didn't expect it to be positive. In fact, it was nasty, which I guess helps you get people to read your reviews. While you are entitled to your opinion, and basically I asked for it, I wish you would give more intelligent thought to what you write. Read my bio and give me some credit for spending a lot of time working on this show. Remember that I gave it a lot of thought and carefully chose every moment for specific reasons.

Being human, I make mistakes. Sometimes I even have bad nights. Get inside my head as best you can, try to figure out what I was trying to do, and then you are free to conjecture about where I might have gone wrong or why you didn't connect with what I'm doing—or even why most of the rest of the audience did.

Instead you assumed that I spent years training and months rehearsing just so I could waste your time and cheat audiences out of their money. You attacked me personally as if "I" am only this show, this performance, this opinion you have. This hurts me. It does not make my show better or me better. But maybe you can learn from this review I've just written.

Not amused,
Allen

Often experts will criticize not only us but our entire group, dismissing all country-western singers, all textile artists, or all rhyming poets while getting in their digs at us. Joan, a painter, responded to this combination of personal criticism and group criticism in the following way:

Dear Mr. Curator Critic,

I thank you for your candor in replying to my inquiry for consideration in the exhibition. However, I take issue with your reasons for disqualifying me and 349 other artists simply because we participated in the Street Art Projects. As a professional working artist for twenty-six years, I have participated in various events citywide that promote the arts. You take issue with these programs that support artists and raise money for arts programming, but that is no reason to bar all artists who participate in these programs from the exhibition.

It is one thing to state your disagreement with a sponsoring organization and a totally different thing to blackball participating artists because we participated in a program that you must view as either crass or kitschy. I feel that which fund-raiser an artist participates in should not be a standard of consideration. You yourself claim that you advocate the arts community whenever you can. I ask you to support local artists by opening your eyes to what they are creating in their studios, not by which fund-raiser they happen to support.

Sincerely,
Joan

Avoid Giving Their Opinion More Weight than It Deserves

Sometimes we turn to an expert in our field in the hopes of being helped and mentored. If we are rebuffed by that expert, we are inclined to take that rebuff as implied criticism. Shirley had that reaction to being refused admittance to a well-known poets' seminar. She took that rebuff not only as criticism of her poetry but as criticism of her gender and her race as well:

Dear Robert Lowell,

You rejected my request to join your poetry seminar but never told me what was wrong with my poetry, why it did not measure up to your standards. Back then I knew you only as a famous poet, but now I know you were an alcoholic and also mentally ill, in and out of hospitals. I also know that you had a deep ambivalence about women and were not thrilled that African-Americans were being welcomed into the educational and artistic circles into which you were born. I know that you had some serious demons, but I don't give a damn. I hope you are rotting in hell! I'm still writing poetry, but I never send it out. Have I let you get the last word on my poetry? Well, I won't! Starting right now I am getting back on the submissions trail.

Still mad as hell,
Shirley

Don't Turn to Self-Criticism

If we ask for an expert's opinion, expect to receive an expert's opinion, or put ourselves in a position to receive an expert's opinion, and then hear nothing, we are likely to experience that silence as criticism. We send out query letters to editors and hear nothing; we feel criticized. We send out screenplays to directors and hear nothing; we feel criticized. No one reviews the book we just had published; we feel criticized. Sometimes that caustic silence occurs even in face-to-face encounters, as it did for Sharon, a painter:

Dear Liz:

Today, when I was in your gallery, I showed you and your assistant digital pictures of my latest work. Your response was no response, except to acknowledge that you saw the pictures. I realize that this new work is different from my usual work, but different is not bad. I have been receiving very positive feedback on this series from fellow artists. Based on previous criticisms from these artists, I know that they are sincere in their positive response to my new paintings.

I am assuming that your nonresponse was a negative one, and I would like to know the reason. Is it that you do not want to comment if you have not seen the actual work? Is it that the work will not fit with what you are showing at your gallery? Do you feel that it is not good work? I am at a loss and feel shut out. Please tell me what you are thinking.

Sincerely,
Sharon

Seek Out Positive Influences

It is also sometimes incumbent upon us to challenge the experts and professional critics in our life, so as to retain our power, redress an injustice, or for some similarly important reason. Janis explained:

Dear Dr. Jones,

After your talk at my college years ago, I challenged you in the discussion period afterward when you stated that a student in one of your classes who could not or would not complete an assignment to your satisfaction was "out" and that you would never negotiate with him or attempt to work with him. I asked if you weren't concerned that you might sometimes be throwing the baby out with the bathwater. Wasn't it possible that a particularly talented student might be the very person unable to fulfill an assigned project because his thought was developing in some other, equally valid direction, a direction that might actually be your duty to support and guide? You responded, "Young woman, you could go a long way in this world, but you never will." The assembled auditorium of students and faculty gasped.

I wasn't as shocked as they were. I have learned, finally and at great cost, that some teachers and mentors are extremely dangerous to their students and protégés. Like abusive parents, they need to prevent the young talent in their temporary charge from blooming because their own wounds and disappointments have made them cruel and have left them with a need to see others suffer. I am glad that we had that exchange, although it had the ferocity of a curse. It and other similar experiences have taught me that I must seek out positive sources of support and that these sources may not be other people. I may find truer help in books, films, music, prayer, and meditation than in the likes of you.

Best,
Janis

Tips for Dealing with Professional Critics

Here are six tips for dealing with the criticism that comes your way from experts and professional critics. Remember that:

- You must remain the final arbiter of the work you do and the life you lead.
- Experts and critics have their agendas and their professional biases. They do not come to their opinions with clean hands.
- It is not unusual for two experts to have different opinions on the same matter and for a third expert to have a third opinion.
- Credentials, expertise, and position do not give experts and critics the right to be rude, cruel, or otherwise tyrannical.

- Experts and critics often have a much smaller, duller, and narrower understanding of matters than their posturing would lead you to believe.
- By the same token, experts and critics may provide you with useful information and even vital information, so their criticism needs to be appraised rather than dismissed out of hand.

Criticism of Your Group

We are each made up of multiple group identities, and every time that group is criticized, we feel criticized. A given person might be a woman, an African-American, a Baptist, a flower painter, a Democrat, a mother, a southerner, a bisexual, and more, and when one of those groups is criticized she is likely to feel criticized as well.

Criticism of their group affects people deeply. We only have to look at the conflicts between Christians and Jews, Catholics and Protestants, Christians and Moslems, Jews and Arabs, Moslems and Hindus, and so on to recognize how much emotion is generated by virtue of nothing more than group identification. All over the world, and from the beginning of time, our human ability to hate and to make war has coalesced around the simplest "us and them" sort of mentality. It is therefore no wonder that a criticism of any one of the groups with which you identify—your political group, your religious group, your racial group, your ethnic group, etc.—might hit you hard and stop you in your tracks.

If your group is physically attacked, you have little choice but to stand with your group and help beat back the attack. If Pearl Harbor is bombed, you start fighting the Japanese, the Germans, and the Italians, irrespective of any good feelings you have for the Japanese, the Germans, or the Italians. But what if your group is merely criticized? What if someone tells a kike joke or a nigger joke? What if your new brother-in-law confidentially informs you, "Had a great day! Tough contract negotiation, but I managed to Jew the guy down"? Is this more like Pearl Harbor being bombed or more like a fly landing on your nose? Is it worth saying something? And if you don't say something, will you stew all day about not having said anything?

Confounding the matter further are our own concerns about belonging to this group or that group. We may not like the habits, customs, or practices of our own group but not be able to escape association with that group by virtue of our ethnicity, religious affiliation, or skin color. We may hate having entered into the "too old for hip-hop" or "too old for Hollywood" group and despair about our age as much as we despise those who criticize us for being over the hill. How we react to criticism of our group is made more complicated by the fact that we ourselves may be critical of our group, at least to some extent, self-critical (for instance, about not having made it in hip-hop or Hollywood yet), or both.

Detaching to Deflect

On balance, it is better to detach from our group identifications and not get in an uproar every time a woman, a lesbian, a Jew, an African-American, a southerner, or a country-western singer is criticized. We do this detaching as a natural corollary to working the six keys, by virtue of the fact that we have grown philosophical and phlegmatic, are attuned to our own meaning needs (as opposed to the needs of any group), and are in good charge of our self-talk and personality. Sometimes we make the mindful decision that a certain group criticism must be addressed, for reasons that we deem important and not because we have gotten hot under the collar. Most of the time we decide to let group criticism roll right off our back.

Ralph, a monochromatic painter who painted all-white paintings (perhaps you can feel your own criticism of Ralph and of the very idea of monochromatic painting welling up inside of you), discovered that he could tolerate and even enjoy criticism of his all-white paintings but hated being lumped with classic monochromatic painters, such as Ad Reinhardt and Yves Klein, and associated with their faults, faults Ralph himself considered blameworthy. When I asked him why this group criticism affected him so negatively, he replied, "I don't paint like them, I don't share their faults—I have plenty of my own, but they aren't theirs —and I need my work to be judged on its own merits."

"So it isn't criticism of the group that bothers you," I continued, "but being included in the group at all?"

"It amounts to that, yes."

"But you can't extricate yourself from that group identification, can you? Not while painting all-white paintings?"

"I don't think I can. I tried calling them snow paintings, but that didn't work. Then I tried to make something of the fact that what they were painted on was as important as how they looked. But that didn't take either. I guess I'm a monochromatic painter, pure and simple."

"Then tell me what you want to do when you're lumped in with other monochromatic painters and included in criticisms of them."

Ralph thought about that. "Internally, I want to shrug it off. For the world, I want a simple, clear thing to say that stands for what I'm feeling. Something like 'I'm in the tradition of monochromatic painting, but I paint in my own idiom.' Something like that, only better! I need to craft one really smart sentence and use it in the world as shorthand. For the rest—I'll just have to ignore it."

Because wars are fought over it and because the world may even end as a result of it, we can't take the matter of group identifications and group criticism lightly. Criticism of their group is a hot-button item for most people, which is why most extended family gatherings do not include a single discussion of religion, politics, race, or anything group associated. As emotionally inflammatory as criticism of our group may be, however, we still have the job of deciding which group criticisms we deem important enough to spend our precious time on and which we will let go of instantly. All things being equal, the more criticism we manage to put in the second basket, the better.

Criticism from Strangers

You get on a bus, and the driver looks you up and down and mutters, "You people!" You're in an airport, and the little boy next to you points at you and stage-whispers to his mother, "Why is his belly so big?" You're at a networking luncheon, and people take turns introducing themselves. As you introduce yourself, someone interrupts you with "Can't you speak up? You'll never get anywhere squeaking like that!" Shouldn't criticism of this sort be the easiest to handle, as it comes from strangers who matter to us not one little bit? It should be, and it can be; but it has an element that makes it special: the element of surprise.

It is that element of surprise that rocks us. If we knew that the driver of the next bus had hemorrhoids and was cursing everyone who boarded his bus, we would ignore his criticism when he leveled it at us and we might even smile compassionately. If we knew that one time today—at about noon, at the airport—some little child was going to make a comment about our weight (or our hair, our wrinkles, our outfit, or our skin color), we would feel prepared and would handle the moment with minimal distress. It is the fact that we are unprepared for these surprise stranger criticisms that gives them their power to disturb us and to hurt us.

Be Prepared to "Flip the Switch"

The answer is to *be* prepared. It doesn't take a superhuman, evolved, psychologically rock-steady person to blissfully ignore stranger criticism. It requires only that you stand ready to flip a switch, from vulnerable to invulnerable, from open to closed, from pregnable to impregnable, a switch that you learn to throw in a microsecond, even as the stranger criticism is hitting your ear. This is a variation of your six-key work: this switch controls your attitude, your self-talk, and your personality in such a way that you are able to gain complete control of your mind and your emotions even when you are surprised by a verbal attack from a stranger.

Right now, unless you have been working the six keys, you are geared to hear every criticism that comes your way and take it in too deeply. What if you spent the next month blissfully ignoring every criticism directed at you? At the end of that month, wouldn't you have acquired a whole new attitude? Imagine how much sunnier and saner life would feel if shots like the ones earlier never even registered. When you find yourself in the world, simply say to yourself, "Switch on." By that you mean, "My security system is armed. No matter how craftily I'm ambushed by some stranger criticism, I won't even hear it. It will go directly in one ear and out the other."

I am not advocating that you defend yourself against stranger criticism using psychological defenses like denial, repression, rationalization, or any one of the other score of defenses available to us. Rather, I am advocating an affirmative detachment, where you make a conscious decision to let harmful stranger comments vanish like puffs of smoke. You are quite aware of what you are doing and, because you remain aware, entirely capable of taking in and considering the occasional stranger criticism that you deem important to process. Very few will rise to that level of importance, but when the occasional one does, you stand ready to deal with it.

I had a client, Martinique, practice this "switch on" technique. Most people experience stranger criticism only rarely. Martinique, a dancer, experienced it daily by virtue of the fact that at her day job she worked the express line at a supermarket where they had put in a new computer system that slowed the express line to a crawl. By the time they got to her, virtually every customer had grown impatient and irritable, and some were half-mad with fury.

Before trying the "switch on" technique, Martinique thought she was going to have to quit. The pressure and the level of animosity had grown unbearable. Then she tried this technique. As soon as she took her place at the checkout counter, she said to herself, "Switch on." She could feel herself grow calm, and she discovered that she was actually smiling. By the end of her shift her smile had completely vanished, but she experienced the day as 100 percent less stressful and even felt equal to rushing off to dance class, which she had begun skipping because of work-related stress.

The main power that strangers have is the power to surprise you. There is hardly anything a stranger can say to you that you wouldn't feel equal to ignoring, if only you knew that the criticism was coming. Become better prepared to meet the surprise attacks of strangers by remembering that the unexpected is a commonplace. When you venture into the world, you become a target for the occasional unjust dart. As unexpected as those darts are, they are also entirely predictable.

To consider

- How do you tend to handle indirect or implied criticism? How would you prefer to handle it?
- Do you engage in the kind of work that will bring you into contact with experts and professional critics? Have you thought through how you intend to handle their criticism?

- With what groups do you identify? Are some of those identifications hot-button identifications, such that whenever that group is criticized you get riled up? Would you like to rethink or change your approach to handling criticism of those particular hot-button group identifications?
- When a stranger surprises you with some out-of-the-blue criticism, are you typically little affected or greatly affected? What approach would you like to take to stranger criticism?

To do

- Make a list of the varieties of criticism we've discussed—criticism from family members, loved ones, friends, peers, coworkers, bosses, customers/clients, experts, professional critics, critics of your group, strangers, and yourself—and rank-order this list from easiest to handle to hardest. Do you want to take one approach with your easiest critics and another with your hardest critics, or will one approach (using the six keys) work for all your critics?

11

Working the Toxic Criticism Program

When someone disapproves of you or disapproves of something you have done, we call that disapproval *criticism*. Toxic criticism is disapproval that causes you significant pain, deflects you from your path, or affects your self-image. The most important thing to remember about criticism is that disapproval "out there" can't become toxic "in here" unless we grant it that power. You and I allow criticism to rise to the level of toxicity. When we're rebuked, when our actual or imagined faults are pointed out to us, when our work is knocked, something potentially threatening—to our livelihood, to our sense of self, even to our understanding of the world—has occurred. But how that blow lands is a function of how well you've prepared yourself to deal with criticism.

Use the Tools and Strategies in This Book

You prepare yourself by working the six keys. The first key is the existential key. Until you decide your path in life matters, that it is ultimately your responsibility to live by your cherished principles, and that you and only you can create a life worth living, you will have insufficient motivation to put criticism in its place. You will allow yourself to be bruised and battered by criticism simply because you don't have more important matters to consider.

Knowing your life path, at least in outline, is a crucial step in defeating criticism.

Second, you commit to learning how to appraise situations. To take charge of your life and to stand in appropriate relation to criticism, you need to get in the habit of appraising situations rather than defensively reacting to them. You want to decide whether a criticism rises to a level of importance such that it is worth considering; you want to intuit the contextual nature of the criticism; you want to get a handle on what just transpired. If you can do this right in the moment, that's a bonus, as then you don't have to carry the criticism around with you all day. But if you can't effectively respond in the moment, that's no problem. You simply announce to yourself that you will think about what happened as soon as you get the chance.

At the same time, you begin to shift your attitude. This attitude shift is the third key. A pessimistic, self-critical, world-wary, anxious, sorrowful, passive, defeated attitude does not feel good and does not serve you. Your better bet, both with respect to handling criticism and with respect to living your life in general, is to adopt an attitude at once positive and affirmative, so that you look forward to life and feel equal to life's challenges, and also philosophical and phlegmatic, so that much of life's petty annoyances and criticisms roll right off your back. With this attitude in place, you begin to believe in yourself, in your choices, and in your ability to right your ship should you veer off course.

You also want to gain control of your mind and master the art of bringing your self-talk in line with your intentions. This is the fourth key. Because you have come to understand your path and what is true for you, a large percentage of the criticism directed your way will never actually reach you, stopped in its tracks by the strength of your convictions. Because of your new phlegmatic, philosophical attitude, another percentage of criticism will roll off your back. But some criticism will rise to the level of significance and will require your attention, and a lot of the criticism you receive will hurt, even if you know to ignore it. You therefore want to master your self-talk so as to moderate what you say to yourself and not inflame the situation.

The fifth key is maintaining self-awareness about your personality, including a real awareness of your personal defensive style and the ways you typically react in difficult situations. When you're criticized, do you act aggressively, stick your fingers in your ears, or instantly feel shamed and humiliated? Do you have an addictive streak, a depressive streak, an obsessive-compulsive streak? The better you understand yourself and the more you effect change in the direction you determine you ought to move, the happier you will be in general and the better equipped you will be to deal with criticism strategically rather than defensively.

These positive changes are among the behaviors that make up the sixth key. Responding to criticism involves taking mindful action, sometimes in the form of effectively responding to the critic, just as often in the form of effectively responding to the information embedded in the criticism. You might confront a persistent critic and demand that he desist from criticizing you unfairly. Or you might bravely look an appropriate criticism in the eye and make important changes in your life. A toxic episode must be dealt with actively—or else it is not really being dealt with at all.

Eight Steps to Keep You on the Right Track

These six keys translate into the following eight steps:

1. You gain existential clarity. You know your own path.
2. You adopt a philosophical, phlegmatic attitude that allows criticism to roll off your back.

3. You monitor your self-talk and get in the habit of disputing thoughts that do not serve you.
4. You grow aware of your personality idiosyncrasies and deficiencies and take charge of your personality.
5. When you're criticized, you manage the first wave of emotion coursing through you. Then you opt for thought, rather than feeling, by saying "I need to think about this."
6. If you judge that the criticism does not relate to your life path or is otherwise irrelevant, you ignore it. You toss it away as you would a used tissue.
7. If the criticism is worth considering, you think through what it means and how you want to react strategically.
8. Having thought through what to do, you do it.

"Think" Rather Than "Feel"

An essential component of this program for handling toxic criticism is that you think rather than feel. How is that possible? If your mother screams at you, "You're such a slob!" as you try to eat your dinner, how are you supposed to not feel? If you have to sit there night after night and dinner after dinner hearing the same insulting rebuke, how are you supposed to not feel? If your alcoholic father runs you down every chance he gets, letting you know that you have no smarts, no looks, and no chances, how are you supposed to not feel? As we are built to feel if we are built for anything, how is a person supposed to not feel?

That isn't the goal. The goal isn't to stop feeling. The goal is to become more of a master of your emotions so that you are able to move from raw emotion to measured thought as quickly and as painlessly as you can. You begin to master your emotions as a matter of course as you work the six keys. As you work the attitudinal key and become more philosophical and phlegmatic, you prepare yourself to react much less intensely to criticism. By getting a grip on your mind and your personality, you develop a mind-set and a way of being that is more in your control. By better understanding your path in life and by more fully committing to that path, you are less prone to leap to a large emotion when confronted by everyday criticism.

Your goal is to become a master of your emotions, not to rid yourself of them. Therefore, when you find yourself criticized, and even if you have been assiduously working the six keys, you are likely to experience feelings welling up. That first feeling might be shame, anger, fear, embarrassment, hurt, pained surprise, or some combination of these and other feelings. You may not be able to name the feeling; that doesn't matter. You may feel rocked by the power of the feeling; that, too, doesn't matter. What matters is that you learn that a feeling of this sort can and will pass if you know how to weather it and how to ready yourself for thought.

To help weather that first flush of feeling and to help it pass as quickly and as painlessly as possible, try the following three things:

- **Breathe the pain away.** Take several deep breaths, each five seconds on the inhale and five seconds on the exhale. These deep breaths will calm you and give you the chance to let the pain begin to escape from your system. As you breathe deeply, tap into your intuition and gauge whether you feel equal to appraising this criticism on the spot. If you find that you can respond strategically, do so. If you find that you had better wait, muster your strength and say, "Let me get back to you on that." (For more on breathing pain away, please consult *Ten Zen Seconds*.)
- **Think an affirmative thought.** Remember to tell yourself that you are still OK despite having just received a disapproving blow. Have an affirmation or mantra ready at all times that your mind can go to automatically when you find yourself attacked. Your mantra might be "I am perfectly fine," "This is a small mat-

ter on my life path," or "I know how to put opinions in their place." Create a resonant, personalized affirmation that will help you retain your strength and your sense of self when and if someone criticizes you.

• **Remind yourself that you can process your feelings later.** Remind yourself that even if you decide you must stuff your feelings right now so as to respond diplomatically, you will be able to deal with those feelings later on and be able to vent using the "Dear critic" letter-writing approach or some other approach. Let the wash of emotion pass right through you as you tell yourself, "I'll deal with the feelings later. Right now, my goal is to stay calm." Then, later, make sure you do deal with your residual pent-up feelings.

Deal with Feelings in the Moment

Susan, a novelist, had some good success with her first novel and got a large advance for her second novel. She was proud of both her new novel and the advance she received and was extremely happy with her editor, Leslie, who had purchased the novel, praised it, and seemed to love it. Then one day Susan learned that Leslie had taken a job at another publishing house and Susan was being assigned a new editor. This news disappointed her but gave her no hint of the much more disappointing news to come.

Several weeks later she got a call from her new editor, Maxine, who introduced herself. Then Maxine dropped her bombshell. She intensely disliked Susan's novel and felt inclined to cancel the contract for it. But she wanted to give Susan the chance to tackle a major revision that might—just might—salvage the novel. Was Susan up for that revision, which involved introducing considerably more plot and action, or did she just want to go ahead and have them cancel the contract? Maxine stopped abruptly and handed the ball to Susan.

Susan could hardly believe her ears. She felt like throwing up; she wished this editor dead; and she found herself reeling from the criticism. Was her novel actually that bad? How could that be? The previous editor had loved it and forked out a large advance as proof of that love. Now this! Susan, feverish and ill, awash in terrible emotions, had no idea what to say or what to do. Her head hurt and she feared opening her mouth and saying anything.

"Are you there?" Maxine continued.

"I'm here," Susan managed to mutter.

"I know I'm throwing this at you, but I need to know which way you want to go. If you're not up for a major revision, I need to cancel the contract right now."

Susan realized she had to deal with her feelings at lightning speed and get them out of the way to give herself a chance to think straight. She had to put aside her anger, betrayal, disappointment, and anxiety and respond. She heard herself say to herself, "My writing matters to me. My career matters to me. Be careful here." She took a deep breath and felt herself settle, at least enough to allow her to come a decision.

"Let me think about what you just said," Susan replied. "Let me get back to you. Will tomorrow be OK?"

"Later today would be better."

"Then give me your number and I'll get back to you later today."

When she got off the phone, Susan immediately called Sandy, her literary agent, and explained the situation.

"Something must be going on," Sandy replied. "Maybe they're canceling contracts to save money. If it isn't that, I just don't get it. Everybody there loved your novel. Let me call around."

As she waited for Sandy to get back to her, Susan took stock. To begin with, this amounted to a terrible blow. There was no way to spin this into a blessing or an opportunity. It was bad news, pure and simple, almost the worst news she could have gotten, short of scary news about her health. At the same time, she recognized that not a single bone in her body felt like leaping to the conclusion that Maxine was right about the novel. Maxine might hate it; but Susan did not agree that it was unlovable. It pleased her that the work she had been doing on herself, work equivalent to six keys work, helped prevent her from calling herself names, drifting into the dark side of her personality, or engaging in any self-criticism whatsoever.

An hour later Sandy rang her back.

"I've been calling around," Sandy said. "It looks like they're trying to cancel as many as twenty or thirty contracts to save money. I think this has very little to do with you, but nevertheless you're caught in the middle. I doubt that going forward with the revisions is going to make any difference. What do you think? Do you want to try your hand at the revisions and see how this plays out? Or let them cancel the contract?"

Susan thought about this—surprisingly calmly, it struck her. "The novel is fine," she said after a moment. "Given these circumstances, I can't see revising it. So—I guess the novel is dead?"

"Dead there, maybe," Sandy replied. "But several editors expressed interest in it before we sold it to Leslie. Let me poke around. Don't get back to Maxine until you hear from me. Let me test the waters before you make a decision."

"All right."

As Susan waited to hear back from Sandy, she thought about what had just transpired. In the blink of an eye, a calamity had occurred. Embedded in the calamity, and probably thrown in as a mere excuse, was a jolt of toxic criticism. Why couldn't Maxine have simply and honestly said, "We have been told to save money, so we are canceling many contracts, especially on the riskier books. While we loved your novel, it seems like one of our riskier titles. Therefore, we are dropping it"? Why did Maxine have to disguise the truth and muddy the waters with false criticism, which only made matters harder to comprehend and more hurtful? Susan could only shake her head.

The only solace Susan could take from the situation was that she had handled herself well. She had mastered her feelings in the moment and, as a direct result of that mastery, now had nothing that she regretted saying and nothing that needed undoing. That she had handled herself well was small consolation, but it was important consolation nonetheless. She was glad that she hadn't raced to self-criticism and gotten down on her novel or on herself. She was glad that she had gotten a grip on her mind after the initial pain and confusion had subsided. She was glad that she had handled the incident with as much savvy and assurance as she could muster. Now she waited to hear from her agent whether anything could be salvaged from this catastrophe.

Getting Existential Clarity

It helped that Susan knew her writing and her writing life mattered to her. Criticisms and crises connected to her writing life couldn't be ignored with a cavalier shrug because, in her construction of the universe, writing rose to the level of existential importance. But what if you don't know what really matters to you? What if you aren't sure what your path looks like or what principles you want to uphold? Then stop everything! Because nothing is more important than this first step in the process.

If you are going to live your life in accordance with your life purposes, you had better articulate them, memorize them, and make sure you really believe in them. You need to identify your reasons for living and the role (or roles) you intend to play in life. Your life purposes may be to battle injustice, live a life better than your baser instincts, make beautiful things, do good deeds, and so on. These are the sorts of life purposes that are rich enough and big enough to count. What are yours?

Coming up with just one life purpose will probably not be enough. Take "battling injustice." Can you base a life on that purpose alone? I think not, even as profound a life purpose as "battling injustice" is. It turns out that a person who feels really alive has several life purposes in mind as she proceeds through life. These multiple life purposes can and hopefully will fit together seamlessly into a composite life purpose agenda and might include the following five distinct purposes:

- To make use of your innate talents and abilities, your heart, mind, hands, your very being
- every day
- in the service of truth telling and other important values,
- while at the same getting some real satisfaction out of life
- through love and work.

These combine into a sentence that can become your life purpose statement: "I will make use of myself every day in the service of truth telling and other important values while at the same time getting some real satisfaction out of life through love and work." This is a solid life purpose statement upon which a good life can be built.

However, this may not be *your* life purpose statement. Try your hand at arriving at your own. Spend the next few minutes naming your own life purposes. Remember that you can't know how to contextualize criticism until you know what deep purposes you are intending to serve. Try to articulate those purposes right now. Then, if you can, order them and rank them. Take all the time you need to do this exercise properly, as no exercise you ever attempt will prove more important than this one. Once you have your life purposes named and ranked, create a single sentence of the sort I constructed earlier, a sentence that can and will become your instructions for living.

Then use it. The most straightforward way is to memorize it so it is as readily available as your name, address, and phone number. It is at least that important, more important than your name, really, as your name was given to you and your life purpose statement you actively chose. With it memorized and instantly available, you have a standard by which to judge whether a given criticism can be ignored or must be addressed. Most criticism is of the first variety, so by doing just this one thing you will have eliminated a sizable portion of the toxicity in your life.

If you can't come up with a life purpose statement or you don't want to take the time to craft one, at least try the following. As you go through your day, occasionally ask yourself, "Is what I'm doing at this moment central to my life path, or is it peripheral?" Driving to work might be peripheral; your actual work might be central. Chatting with a relative might be peripheral; chatting with your child might be central. By noticing which activities, events, and interactions are central and which peripheral, you will begin to gain an intuitive understanding of the contours of your path. Then when you're criticized, you'll be able to say internally, "Given my path, this criticism is [or isn't] relevant."

Be Prepared with Appropriate Responses to Criticism

Your response to criticism is in your control and must be in your control. You don't want to operate in a knee-jerk, one-response-fits-all way, whether that one way is to ignore all criticism, always apologize, or always counterattack. You want to have a complete repertoire of responses available to you. There are limitless ways of responding to a given criticism, from ignoring it completely to replying in the moment to replying two days later to changing your life path because of what the criticism revealed. From this limitless array of responses, you choose the response that best serves your interests.

Consider the following scenario. You've been writing short stories for a year or two. Usually editors reject them with a form letter or a brief comment, but today you get the following editorial response on your latest short story: "This isn't a short story at all! It's more like a condensed novel. If these are the kinds of short stories you intend to write, you should stop writing short stories! No one's going to want to publish them or read them."

Let's take a look at how you might think through your response.

"This story has been close to publication at a number of magazines, if I can judge by the favorable comments I've received so far. So I think that I don't believe what this editor has to say. Let me file her comment away and send the story out to the next several places on my list. If it keeps getting rejected, I'll put her criticism back on the table and think about it." Response: you send the story out again without hesitation or further analysis.

"I hate this editor's tone! I would love to give her a piece of my mind and tell her what I think of her magazine, her grandiosity, and her abuse of power. But I know that I'm going to have to deal with editors my whole life if I want to be published, and many of them will say summarily dismissive things of this sort. My best bet is to breathe right through this and accept that I invite criticism by walking this path." Response: you draft a never-mailed "Dear critic" letter so that you can vent and do some further processing.

"I understand that, as a writer, I'm going to have to live with criticism of this sort. But I think that unless I occasionally respond, I am going to lose my power and eventually stop writing. I think this is a case where I would like to respond. I need to tell this editor that she should never tell a person to stop writing, that that is damaging and insulting, and that she can wiggle around all she wants as to 'what she meant' but that, bottom line, she should refrain from saying such things. I need to tell this editor this one time, just to make sure that I don't allow editors to frighten me or cow me." Response: you make an actual reply, one that you carefully craft and intentionally send.

"Her comment about my story being a 'condensed novel' really strikes a chord. I've always wanted to write long fiction, but I think I believed I had to get there gradually, by writing short fiction first. But what if I'm ready to try my hand at a novel and I'm just putting that off because I don't feel confident enough to begin? That feels true. So I guess I need to thank this editor (though I won't!) for pointing this out to me, brace myself, and start on a novel. I wonder: Should I use this story as the starting point? Or should I use one of my other stories? Or should I start from scratch?" Response: you make a conscious shift in your life's work, a shift provoked by criticism.

Each of these is a reasonable response—and each one is completely different. How you respond depends on all the factors we've been discussing, including the facts of the matter, this exact moment on your life path, what in your personality you want to bring forward, and the complete context in which the criticism occurs. It is idle to hope that you can "master" criticism in some simple, foolproof way. That goal makes no sense, because some percentage of the time the criticism you receive will be life-altering and even lifesaving.

Breaking the Cycle

Criticism hurts. Criticism also comes with the territory, especially if we have ambitions. And criticism sometimes contains vital information. If it only hurt, we might plot a course to avoid it. But because it sometimes contains vital information and because we actively invite it into our life if we have ambitions, avoiding it isn't an option. We must deal with the pain it brings and the information it contains. Only then will we feel as if we are living our life richly and authentically.

Here is a last "Dear critic" letter, written by a young painter who overcame toxic criticism in childhood and learned to handle criticism as an adult, including the criticism she invited by virtue of choosing to become an artist.

Dear Toby and Alec:

When I was young, you criticized me. You criticized me about everything. Without going into the exact instances, too many and too painful to mention, I just want you to know that it hurt. I was always forced to protect myself, to defend who I was as a person. I know it was all done under the guise of teasing, and I probably even laughed along with you, but it went to the core. About a year ago I saw an old film clip of myself at a family function. I was so shy, I hardly recognized myself. I didn't remember being that shy. I think that was to escape being noticed, to stay out of the spotlight—in other words, to avoid criticism in front of others.

I know our entire family is competitive. Dad was competitive, and it naturally transferred to you, my brothers. Where does a nonathletic girl fit into this picture? The only way I knew how to fit in was to become the best in something else. I sat first chair after just a short time in the high school band. It was my way of getting recognition for being the best in a way that was possible for me. I loved music, and if I didn't have that throughout my school years, I'm not sure how I would have fared. It was my social life, my success, my love.

When I went on to college, I found a new love, photography. I became very good at it. I almost always brought in the best photographs for critique. There was that competitive thing again! It felt good to be the best. It felt good to be rewarded with praise. I loved it, and I soared after a critique. It was criticism in a positive way and in public. I think this was the beginning of my healing from childhood criticism. I could be critiqued in a positive way, and I learned how to improve without all the negativity.

Now I'm a painter. I love having shows and having people tell me they enjoy my work. It's wonderful. My spirit soars, and I love the feeling. I wish I could have had that when I was young, and I wonder how I would be different today. Now that I am away from the toxic environment of childhood, I can handle criticism and I can shine. I hope that you, too, have grown and realize that there is more to life than tearing down others so as to build yourselves up. Lots of people can "win."

Your sister,
Denise

This is the journey that each of us is on. We start out unequal to the challenges that toxic criticism presents and incline toward ineffective, sometimes self-destructive ways of handling that criticism. Then if we are lucky and brave, we grow mindful of the path we want to walk and adept at overcoming obstacles on that path. We recognize the extent to which we let the comments of others circulate as toxins in our system and learn how to respond strategically to that portion of criticism that can't be ignored. Even after all this, some criticism is bound to hurt. But we are thrilled to discover that it is within our power to transform criticism from something toxic and destructive to something completely manageable.

To consider

- What one thing will you take away from this book and make your own so as to improve your chances of handling criticism effectively?

- What remains your biggest challenge to handling criticism effectively? What would you like to try to do to meet that challenge?

To do

- If you haven't done so already, think through and prepare your life purpose statement.
- Reread and write out the eight steps that appear in this chapter. See if you can put them into practice.

Additional Reading

Axelrod, Alan. *201 Ways to Deal with Difficult People*. New York: McGraw-Hill, 1997.

Bergner, Raymond. *Pathological Self-Criticism*. New York: Springer, 1995.

Bernstein, Albert. *Emotional Vampires*. New York: McGraw-Hill, 2002.

Bloomfield, Harold. *Making Peace with Yourself*. New York: Ballantine Books, 1996.

Bolton, Robert. *People Skills*. New York: Touchstone, 1986.

Brown, Nina. *Children of the Self-Absorbed*. Oakland: New Harbinger Publications, 2001.

Carter, Jay. *Nasty Bosses*. Chicago: McGraw-Hill, 2004.

Carter, Jay. *Nasty People*. Chicago: McGraw-Hill, 2003.

Cava, Roberta. *Dealing with Difficult People*. Willowdale, ON: Firefly Books, Ltd., 2004.

Cavaiola, Alan, and Lavender, Neil. *Toxic Coworkers*. Oakland: New Harbinger Publications, 2000.

Carson, Rick. *Taming Your Gremlin*. New York: Perennial Currents, 2003.

Crowe, Sandra. *Since Strangling Isn't an Option*. New York: Perigee, 1999.

Elgin, Suzette Haden. *The Gentle Art of Verbal Self-Defense at Work*. Parasmus, NJ: Prentice Hall Press, 2000.

Elliott, James. *Disarming Your Inner Critic*. Lafayette, LA: Anthetics Institute Press, 1999.

Ellis, Albert, and Powers, Marcia Grad. *The Secret of Overcoming Verbal Abuse*. Chatsworth, CA: Wilshire Book Company, 2000.

Engel, Beverly. *The Emotionally Abusive Relationship*. New York: John Wiley, 2003.

Evans, Patricia. *The Verbally Abusive Relationship*. Holbrook, MA: Adams Media Corporation, 1996.

Forward, Susan. *Emotional Blackmail*. New York: Harper Paperbacks, 1998.

Forward, Susan. *Toxic In-Laws*. New York: Harper Paperbacks, 2002.

Forward, Susan. *Toxic Parents*. New York: Bantam, 2002.

Genua, Robert. *Managing Your Mouth*. New York: American Management Association, 1993.

Glass, Lillian. *Toxic People*. New York: St. Martin's Griffin, 1997.

Heldmann, Mary Lynne. *When Words Hurt*. New York: Ballantine Books, 1989.

Horn, Sam. *Tongue Fu!* New York: St. Martin's Griffin, 1997.

Hotchkiss, Sandy. *Why Is It Always About You?* New York: Free Press, 2003.

Ignoffo, Matthew. *Coping with Your Inner Critic*. New York: Rosen Publishing Group, 1989.

Lloyd, Ken. *Jerks at Work*. Franklin Lakes, NJ: Career Press, 1999.

Lubit, Roy. *Coping with Toxic Managers, Subordinates . . . and Other Difficult People*. Parasmus, NJ: Prentice Hall, 2003.

Maisel, Eric. *Coaching the Artist Within*. Novato, CA: New World Library, 2005.

Maisel, Eric. *Ten Zen Seconds*. Naperville, IL: Sourcebooks, 2007.

Maisel, Eric. *The Van Gogh Blues*. Emmaus, PA: Rodale, 2002.

McKay, Matthew. *Messages: The Communications Skills Book*. Oakland, CA: New Harbinger Publications, 1995.

Namie, Gary. *The Bully at Work*. Naperville, IL: Sourcebooks, 2000.

Neuharth, Dan. *If You Had Controlling Parents*. New York: Harper Paperbacks, 1999.

Newman, John. *How to Stay Cool, Calm & Collected When the Pressure's On*. New York: American Management Association, 1992.

Scott, Gini Graham. *A Survival Guide for Working with Humans*. New York: Amacom, 2004.

Stone, Hal, and Stone, Sidra. *Embracing Your Inner Critic: Turning Self-Criticism into a Creative Asset*. San Francisco: Harper San Francisco, 1993.

Stout, Martha. *The Sociopath Next Door*. New York: Broadway Books, 2005.

Tingley, Judith. *Say What You Mean, Get What You Want*. New York: American Management Association, 1996.

Toropov, Brandon. *The Complete Idiot's Guide to Getting Along with Difficult People*. New York: Alpha Books, 1997.

Weisinger, Hendrie. *The Power of Positive Criticism*. New York: American Management Association, 1999.

Weiss, Donald. *Why Didn't I Say That?!* New York: American Management Association, 1996.

Index

About the Author

Eric Maisel, Ph.D., is a licensed family therapist, creativity coach, and creativity coach trainer with a doctorate in counseling psychology and master's degrees in creative writing and counseling. His more than twenty-five works of nonfiction and fiction include *The Van Gogh Blues*, a Books for a Better Life Award finalist; *Affirmations for Artists*, named best book of the year for artists by *New Age Magazine*; *Fearless Creating*; *The Creativity Book*; and the recently published *Coaching the Artist Within*, *A Writer's Paris*, and *A Writer's San Francisco*.

A regular contributor to *Writer's Digest* and *The Writer Magazine*, Maisel writes a monthly "Coaching the Artist Within" column for *Art Calendar Magazine* and founded and wrote *Callboard Magazine*'s "Staying Sane in the Theater" column. Regarded as America's foremost creativity coach, Maisel maintains a private creativity coaching practice in San Francisco and trains creativity coaches nationally and internationally.

You can learn more about Dr. Maisel's books and creativity coaching services at ericmaisel.com, and you can contact him at ericmaisel@hotmail.com.